172

The Critical Idiom

General Editor: JOHN D. JUMP

8 *Metre, Rhyme and Free Verse*

Metre, Rhyme and Free Verse / *G. S. Fraser*

Methuen & Co. Ltd

First published 1970
by Methuen & Co Ltd
11 New Fetter Lane London EC4

© 1970 G. S. Fraser

Printed in Great Britain
by Cox & Wyman Ltd, Fakenham, Norfolk

SBN 416 17290 3   Hardback
SBN 416 17300 4   Paperback

*This title is available in both hard and paperback
editions. The paperback edition is sold subject to
the condition that it shall not by way of trade or
otherwise, be lent, re-sold, hired out, or
otherwise circulated without the publisher's prior
consent in any form of binding or cover other than
that in which it is published and without a similar
condition including this condition being imposed
on the subsequent purchaser.*

Distributed in the U.S.A.
by Barnes & Noble Inc.

Contents

General Editor's Preface

This volume is one of a series of short studies, each dealing with a single key item, or a group of two or three key items, in our critical vocabulary. The purpose of the series differs from that served by the standard glossaries of literary terms. Many terms are adequately defined for the needs of students by the brief entries in these glossaries, and such terms will not be the subjects of studies in the present series. But there are other terms which cannot be made familiar by means of compact definitions. Students need to grow accustomed to them through simple and straightforward but reasonably full discussions of them. The purpose of this series is to provide such discussions.

Some of the terms in question refer to literary movements (e.g., 'Romanticism', 'Aestheticism', etc.), others to literary kinds (e.g., 'Comedy', 'Epic', etc.), and still others to stylistic features (e.g., 'Irony', 'The Conceit', etc.). Because of this diversity of subject-matter, no attempt has been made to impose a uniform pattern upon the studies. But all authors have tried to provide as full illustrative quotation as possible, to make reference whenever appropriate to more than one literature, and to compose their studies in such a way as to guide readers towards the short bibliographies in which they have made suggestions for further reading.

John D. Jump

University of Manchester

Acknowledgements

I should like to thank the General Editor for his detailed help and advice both at the typescript and proof stages; Mrs Sheila Dewhurst for her intelligent and ruthless cutting down of a typescript draft that was a third too long; and my Leicester colleague Philip Collins for making the index.

I owe a great deal to conversations over a great many years about metrics with poets and scholars: among whom I would mention I. A. Richards, William Empson, Richard Murphy, Hilary Corke, Edward Lucie-Smith, George Macbeth, B. S. Johnson, and Terence Hawkes.

I

Some Definitions and Distinctions

When we stand on the sea-shore, and watch waves breaking on the sand and being sucked out again, there is a basic similarity in the motion of each wave, but no two waves break in a manner that is absolutely identical. This similarity in difference of the motion of waves we could call rhythm. There is a similar phenomenon, not only very obviously in successive lines of verse, but also in written prose and in spoken speech, at all its various levels of formality and informality. In a good writer or a good speaker, we notice something that can be called a distinctive rhythm; but even in clumsy writing and hesitant speech there is rhythm of a sort. Orators and writers of imaginative or emotionally persuasive prose pay a good deal of conscious attention to their rhythms. In plain expository prose, such as this book is written in, both writer and reader are consciously concerned not mainly with rhythm but with sense. Nevertheless, our sense of a prose writer's rhythm, however little, it is a fully conscious sense, affects our pleasure in reading him and our ease in understanding him. A succession of sentences too much of the same length, or too much in the same pattern, tends to weary us, however clear the writer's meaning is; on the other hand, a pleasing modulation of rhythms, as in a philosopher like Bishop Berkeley, can help us to follow with pleasure trains of argument that, less gracefully expressed, we might find remote and abstruse.

The difference between verse and prose or speech, therefore, is not that verse has rhythm, and prose and speech have not, but that in <u>verse a rhythmical unit</u>, the line, is superimposed upon the general grammatical unit of all discourse, the sentence. Prose is written in sentences. Verse is written in sentences and also in lines. A succession of lines of the same metrical pattern, a succession of iambic pentameters, for instance, is rather like a succession of waves breaking on the shore. Each has a similar pattern, which can be measured, but none is absolutely identical with any other. Indeed, the *same* line of verse occurring in different places in a poem – a refrain at the end of a stanza, say, or Mark Antony's repeated

> For Brutus is an honourable man –

is never exactly rhythmically identical. It is scanned in exactly the same way, but it does not *sound* exactly the same, or it is not *performed* in exactly the same way. The rules of scansion can, as it were, give us the broad wave pattern but, without a great deal of elaboration and complication in our system of notation, they cannot define the individual wave.

Metrics, in the fairly simple sense with which it is being handled in this primer, is concerned with the recognition and naming of broad wave patterns in lines of verse. A knowledge of metrics can stop us from reading a line of verse aloud wrongly; but it will not necessarily enable us to read a line of verse aloud in the most effective way. It provides, as it were, a sense of a skeletal structure, upon which the good performer has to put flesh and blood.

ANALYSING A LINE OF VERSE

Both prose and verse, then, have rhythm, but the rhythm of good prose is very various, and too much monotony or repetition is a fault in prose rhythm: a writer like Charles Dickens tends to fall into passages of concealed blank verse in his more emotional moments, and the thudding regularity casts doubt on his sincerity.

A writer of verse, on the other hand, by setting out his poem on the page in lines announces to us that he is allowing himself much less scope and variety of rhythmical choice than a writer of prose; and he shows his skill by repeating again and again the same broad rhythmical pattern while at the same time avoiding, by all kinds of subtle contrivances, an impression of mechanical monotony.

A line of verse then is a rhythmical unit, which can be analysed in some way, and which sets up an expectation that it will be followed by a number of similar rhythmical units. We can all recognize such units, but writers on metre have disagreed very much about the proper mode of analysis. Let us take two very famous lines from the beginning of a Shakespeare sonnet:

1 2 3 4 5 6 7 8 9 10
Shall I compare thee to a summer's day?
1 2 3 4 5 6 7 8 9 10
Thou art more lovely and more temperate.

Each of these lines has ten syllables and there are languages, like French and Japanese, in which metrics is based upon syllable count. One should say, in passing, here, that the syllable is a concept belonging to rhetoric or literary discourse rather than to strictly scientific phonetics. In a word like 'distress' it does not matter, metrically, whether we divide it syllabically as 'dis/tress' or 'dist/ress': we are always certain in English where the centre of a syllable is, though we might disagree about its borders. In verse a phrase like 'man/y a' or an adjective like 'fur/ious' is counted as two syllables, though in speech many of us would think of both examples as three syllables, the middle one very short. A native speaker of English, acquainted with English poetry, has no difficulty in recognizing what he means by a syllable in the metrical sense.

Nevertheless, to describe the two Shakespeare lines as merely ten-syllable lines will not do as a definition. We can prove this simply by altering the order of the words in the lines, without changing the sense:

> To a summer's day shall I compare thee?
> More lovely thou art and more temperate.

We have the rhythms now not of verse, but of prose. Many modern poets, as we shall see in a later chapter, are today trying to base their verse on pure syllable count, but I shall argue that their success, when they are successful, relies on the syllable count being reinforced by other concealed regularities, of stress, quantity, pause, or even weak accentual feet. It is *just* possible that Shakespeare's lines as I have turned them around could be used to set up a new pattern of purely syllabic metrical expectation, but I think it would be very difficult.

Another possible way to analyse these lines of Shakespeare's is musically. The pentameter, Geoffrey N. Leech suggests in his interesting recent book *A Linguistic Guide to English Poetry*, is best analysed as a hexameter with a silent stress at the end, which marks the end for the hearer:

> Shall/ Í com/páre thee/ tó a/ súmmer's/ dáy,/^
> Thou/ árt more/ lóvely/^ and móre/témper/ áte/^

The little mark for a silent stress suggests a pause which is musically equivalent to a stress: we pause as it were imperceptibly after 'lovely' and do not crassly make our emphasis 'ánd more': and the silent stress at the end of the line marks our sense, of the closure of a musical unit. Many metrists, since the American Southern poet of the Civil War period, Sidney Lanier, have been attracted by this idea of scanning verse in musical bars. It works perfectly well, but my objection to it is that it suggests a setting for music rather than an analysis of its speech rhythms. It does not help us very much to relate metre to sense. I am mentioning musical scansion here, and then leaving it be, partly because I have a poor musical ear: but partly because I think that most great English poetry approximates to speech rather than to song, and that it is more important to relate metrical patterns in poetry to patterns of meaning – speech meaning, sentence meaning – than to purely musical patterns.

Suppose then that we take an opposite course and assume that the metrical pattern of these two lines is based on speech pattern. One of the most distinctive characteristics of English speech pattern is the phenomenon of stress. We can all recognize a syllable, and distinguish, if we are native English speakers, between 'cónvîct', the noun, and 'cônvíct', the verb, say, because the stress patterns of the two words are opposite. We make other distinctions, for instance between the quantity, or length, of various syllables: *bid*, for instance, is longer than *bit*, and *bide* is longer than *bid*. But differences of quantity do not make a difference usually in sense, or metrically.

We have been assuming in the last paragraph that in marking stress differences in words, there are only two degrees of difference in stress – unstress or minimum stress marked ° and stress, marked '. But the polysyllabic word 'hospitable', whether pronounced in the northern or southern way should convince us that we need at least three degrees of stress. In the southern pronunciation, these could be marked 'hóspîtàblê', with the last short syllable slightly stronger than the second last. Modern phonologists of the Trager-Smith school detect, in fact, not merely three but four degrees of stress differentiation in English word and phrase stress. The mnemonic for this rule is the American phrase foɪ a liftman, 'elevator-operator', which can be scanned thus:

élêvâtôr-òpêrâtôr

or if we use numbers instead of symbols on top of the vocalic part of the syllable, numbers from 1 to 4 indicating degrees of mounting stress:

4 1 2 1 3 1 2 1
elevator-operator.

Shall Í compáre thee: to a súmmer's dáy?
Thou art móre lóvely: and móre témperate.

The colon there is used to indicate a natural sense- and breath-pause in the line, sometimes called the caesura. Analysed for sense stress in this way, Shakespeare's lines look very like old English or medieval alliterative poetry, which consists of a line of two half-lines, each with two syllables of strong sense stress, with a sharp break in the middle, with the difference that the alliterative half-lines are linked by alliteration:

In a *s*ómer *s*éason: whanne *s*óft was the *s*únne . . .

The alliterative linking was necessary to isolate and define the Anglo-Saxon and medieval alliterative line, whose stress patterns, but for this isolation and definition, were exactly the same as prose. Pure stress rhythm is more natural to English than stress-syllable rhythm, and in any good performance of Shakespeare, for instance, we rarely *hear* consciously more than four sense stresses in a metrically five-stressed line:

I come to búry Cáesar nót to práise him.

But the combination of the natural sentence stress pattern and the superimposed pattern of metrical stress makes possible more subtle modulations of sound, sense, pace and feeling than pure stress metre can by itself easily achieve.

We have seen then that in attempting to analyse metrically what all recognize as a line of English verse we are driven to consider in turn pure syllable count, a rather abstract musical bar scheme imposed on the syllable count rather than emerging from it, the phenomenon of stress in English words and phrases (including the number of degrees of stress in spoken English), and the wider pattern of sense-stress or sentence stress. All these approaches seem to give us clues, to have some relevance to how we should analyse these Shakespeare lines, but none seems quite sufficient in itself. So we come round at last to the traditional mode of scansion in iambic feet.

An iambic foot is a metrical unit of two syllables, of which the first syllable is less heavily stressed than the second. But since there are four degrees of stress in English, it is quite possible, for instance, for the first syllable of an iambic foot in any place but the first place in a five-foot line to be stronger than the last syllable in the foot that precedes it. The pattern of expectation set up by the iambic pattern makes possible also, among the many combinations of the four degrees of stress, a foot or two apparently primary stresses, 'Dark dark' or of two apparently very weak stresses 'it is': metrically, and usually also from sentence stress, the second syllable gathers on it the ictus, the bump, the purely metrical stress.

Let us look at the quatrain from Shakespeare analysed into lines of five feet, with indications of the four degrees of stress: using first the symbols, and then the numbers, and also using the colon to indicate the breath or sense break in the line:

> Shàll Í/ cŏmpáre/ thêe: tô/ ă súm/mĕr's dáy?
> Thòu árt/mòre lóve/lȳ: ànd/ mòre témp/ ĕrâte.
> Roùgh wínds/ dŏ sháke/: thĕ dár/lĭng búds/ ŏf Máy
> Ånd súm/mĕr's leáse/: hâth áll/ tôo shórt/ ă dáte.

>   3 4 1 4   1   2 1 4   1   4
> Shall I/compare/ thee: to/ a sum/mer's day?
>   3   4 3   4   1 2   3   4   2
> Thou art/more love/ly: and/ more temp/ĕrate.
>   3   4   1   4   1   4 1   4   1 4
> Rough winds/ do shake/: the dar/ling buds/ of May

ɪ   4   ɪ   4   2   4   2   4   ɪ   4
And sum/mer's lease/: hath all/too short/ a date.

It should be noted that in the first three lines of this quatrain a sensitive reader of poetry might, without any effect of metrical jarring, reverse the feet as marked above:

Sháll Ì . . .
Thóu àrt . . .
Róugh wìnds . . .

This reversal is common and acceptable at the beginning of an iambic pentameter line, and the sentence stress does not jar if the second syllable of the trochee, as the reversed iambus is called, is of almost but not quite equal weight with the first. We can here bring in another factor which has some relevance to English scansion, the factor of quantity, or length of syllable. If we scan 'Sháll Ì' as an accentual trochee, 'shall' is long: if we scan it as an accentual iambic foot, it becomes shorter, almost 'Sh'll Í'. or even 'Sh'll Í' or 'Sh'll Í'. 'Thou' is quantitatively longer in itself than 'art', and we can scan 'Thòu árt' as an accentual iambic foot overlaid on a quantitative trochee: 'Thōu árt . . .' Classical verse differs from English verse in that the verse line is very often, though not always, not a succession of feet of the same kind but a combination of feet of different kinds, the feet being defined quantitatively. It is possible to write English verse quantitatively, and also to imitate classical metres in accentual or stress-syllable feet. And there are stress-syllable equivalents for most classical feet except, possibly, the pyrrhic ° ° and the spondee ‾ ‾. In the Shakespeare quatrain we have been considering 'Shāll Í' could be pronounced with an equal lingering on both words and so could 'Thōu ārt' and 'Rōugh wīnds': and 'thĕe tŏ', a difficult foot for accentual scansion, could be treated, as indicated here, as a quantitative pyrrhic. The Trager-Smith argument against true pyrrhics or spondees in English is that accentually, in the pattern of iambic verse, one syllable of an iambic or trochaic foot must always have at least a very slightly greater stress than the other, or that if two adjacent syllables are to have exactly equal stress there must be a tiny breath-pause between them. We can, nevertheless, attempt to scan Shakespeare's quatrain quantitatively, and note where the quantitative scansion coincides with and where it contradicts the stress-syllable scansion:

> Shāll Ĭ/ cŏmpāre/ thĕe tŏ/ ă sūm/mĕr's dāy?
> Thōu ārt/ mōre lŏve/lў ānd/ mōre tēmp/ ĕrăte.
> Rōūgh wīnds/ dŏ shāke/ thĕ dārl/ĭng būds/ ŏf Māy
> Ănd sūm/mĕr's lēāse/ hăth āll/ tōo shōrt/ ă dāte.

Our uncertainty about whether, in the stress-syllable system, to take 'Shall I', 'Thou art', and 'Rough winds' as iambic or trochaic feet has something to do with the fact that quantitatively they are, or can be read without distorting sense, as spondees. The fact that the last two syllables of 'temperate' are quantitatively a pyrrhic helps to explain why a good reader takes 'temperate' and 'date' as a full rhyme only to the eye, and in fact says something like 'témpĕrît': the reading 'témpĕráte' which would give a full rhyme is aesthetically impossible.

It is possible to analyse any line of English verse quantitatively, and the elements of stress-contrast and of hurrying-lingering contrast – the accentual and the quantitative elements – can please the ear both where they fully coincide and where they fail to do so. There is a famous line of Milton's, from *Lycidas*, whose scansion has been much discussed:

> Weep no/ more, woe/ ful Shep/ herds weep/ no more

With a trochaic opening, which is ordinary and legitimate, this scans:

> Wéep nŏ/ mŏre, wóe/ fŭl Shép/ hĕrds wéep/ nŏ móre.

B

Or in the Trager-Smith system, it could be scanned:

> Wéep nò/ mòre, wóe/ fùl Shép/ hèrds wéep/ nò móre.

But more pleasing to the ear, since it does not mechanically repeat the cadence of 'Weep no more' at the beginning and the end of the line is the perfectly regular iambic scansion:

> Weĕp nó/ mòre, wóe/ fùl Shép/hĕrds, wéep/ nŏ móre.

or, in Trager-Smith scansion.

> Weèp nó/ mòre, wóe/fùl Shép/ hèrds, wéep/ nò móre.

It helps us, I think, to appreciate the music of this line of verse, and also to make up our minds about which of the alternative stress-syllable scansions we prefer, if we also scan it quantitatively:

> W͞eep nō/ mōre, w͞oe/ fùl Sh͞ep/ hĕrds, w͞eep/ nō mōre.

The three quantitative spondees help to slow the line down, and to give it its grave beauty.

After such a long consideration of four very beautiful lines of Shakespeare's we find that it is possible, putting aside the Trager-Smith system, and using the simple binary unstress-stress system to which we are accustomed, to scan them as mechanically regular:

> Shăll Í/ cŏmpáre/ thĕe tó/ ă súm/mĕr's dáy?
> Thoŭ árt/ mŏre lóve/lў ánd/ mŏre témp/ĕráte.
> Roŭgh wínds/ dŏ sháke/ thĕ dárl/ĭng búds/ ŏf Máy
> Ānd súm/mĕr's léase/ hăth áll/ toŏ shórt/ ă dáte.

Our examination, however, of degrees of stress in words and phrases, of sentence-stress or sense-stress patterns, and of quantitative feet as coinciding or not coinciding with stress-syllable feet, should have shown us that this possibility of apparently mechanical scansion does not mean that there is anything mechanical about the rhythm of a poem. There is often a danger, when a line has a striking emotional effect, of assuming that this depends on some striking metrical irregularity. John Donne was a poet who was reproached by his contemporary Ben Jonson for 'not keeping of accent', and it is often assumed that therefore no regular metrical pattern should be sought in his verse. In fact, his metres are basically iambic, and the 'wrenching of accent' comes, usually, not from any metrical carelessness but from unusual sense stresses. In his wonderful poem, *A Valediction: Of Weeping*, I have known good critics scan this line, in a basically iambic poem, as suddenly dactylic:

> Wéep mĕ nŏt/ déad ĭn thĭne/ árms bŭt fŏr/beár (° °)
> Tŏ teách/ thĕ séa/ whăt ĭt/ măy dó/ tŏð sóon . . .

The proper scansion is, of course.

> Weĕp *mé*/ nŏt déad/ iñ *thíne*/aŕms, bút/ fŏrbéar . . .

The whole poem has been about *me* and *thee*, and the metrical emphasis on 'me' and 'thine' here coincides with the proper rhetorical emphasis. In the second of the lines quoted it may be noted that 'toŏ sóon', a regular iambic foot on the stress-syllable system, is a very sonorous spondee, 'tōo sōon', on the quantitative system: a good reader will let us hear the wind soughing.

To distinguish between rhetorical emphasis and metrical emphasis, and to see that one does not have to throw one out of the window in order to do justice to the other, is perhaps the most essential foundation for a proper appreciation of English verse. It has been my aim in this first chapter to bring the reader round to something that he knows already; and to make him realize that the implications of what he knows already are much more complex than he thinks. Simple binary stress-syllable scansion can prevent us from reading a line aloud, or sounding it in our heads, *wrong*: it cannot help us to read the line aloud, or sound it in our heads, strikingly right. But when we supplement it with sense-stress analysis, four-stress foot scansion, and quantitative scansion, our analysis, though more laborious and often more hesitant, can get us much nearer to a proper inner or outer performance of poetry. Just as I have rather by-passed the musical scansion of verse, so I have nothing in this chapter about pitch or intonation the rising and falling tunes for questioning, doubt and assertion that are built into the prosody of the English language. Their notation is too complex for a primer of this sort, and though they have a great deal to do with the effective performance of verse, they hardly bear directly on scansion. Nevertheless, necessarily summary as the definitions and distinctions in this first chapter have been, I think that the reader who has followed them should find the rest of the book much easier. I shall from now on be applying the principles I have worked out to examples, not introducing new principles.

2
Pure Stress Metres

The earliest metre in English and the most natural to the language is pure stress metre. Lines in pure stress metre have an equal number of stresses, primary stresses of the sense-stress sort, but not necessarily an equal number of syllables and they do not divide into feet. There are no fixed rules about how near or how far away from each other syllables of main stress must be. The stress pattern of pure stress verse is, in fact, exactly the same as the stress pattern of natural speech or informal prose, as in Anglo-Saxon poetry and Middle English alliterative poetry (see page 6). The possible pause, sometimes called the caesura, in lines of stress-syllable metre is not an intrinsic part of stress-syllable metre in the same way, and does not have to be marked in scansion. It need not occur in any fixed place in the iambic pentameter line, it can occur in more than one place, and it need not occur at all. In these two lines at the end of Philip Larkin's fine poem in iambic pentameters, 'Church Going', the first line has two breath-pauses, or caesuras, the second has none.

Whích,/ wě ońce heárd/wǎs próp/ěr tó/grǒw wíse (in),
Ǐf ón/ lǐ thát/ sǒ mán/ ǐ deád/ liě róund.

The commas mark the two breath-pauses in the first line and in the stress-syllable line the breath-pause, like punctuation generally, is essentially a device of rhetoric rather than metrics. The first line there is relevant to our remarks in the last chapter about the possibility, or impossibility, of the pyrrhic foot ° ° and the spondee ′ ′ in stress-syllable metre. A fine poet and a good and subtle metrical theorist, John Crowe Ransom, would scan such a line like this:

Whičh, wé/onče héard/ wǎs próp/ěr tǒ/grów wíse (in)

but in fact, if we listen carefully, 'to' is just a little stronger than '-er' and 'wise', because of sense as well as metre, is certainly stronger than 'grow'. On the other hand, if we chose to scan this line *quantitatively*, the last two feet are *certainly* a pyrrhic followed by a spondee:

. . ./ěr tǒ/grōw wīse (in)

Before leaving this Larkin example, I should add that the bracket at the end round the word 'in' is to indicate that this is a weak or feminine ending to the line, which does not count in the scansion of the foot.

This complicated example of stress-syllable scansion, with underlying attention to quantity, should make pure stress scansion, to which we are now coming, seem in comparison a delightfully simple subject. Stress-syllable scansion raises all sorts of problems even for the native English speaker but in pure stress scansion the native English speaker cannot go wrong: the syllables that he stresses for sense are the syllables that are metrically significant. We can scan this moving passage from Langland's *Piers Plowman* immediately, if we bear in mind that in fourteenth-century English the *k* in the word 'knee' was pronounced audibly:

> Yet I cúrbed on my knées: and críed her of gráce,
> And said, 'mércy, Mádam': for Máry, love of Héaven,
> That bòre that blíssful báirn: that bóught us on the Róod,
> Kén me by some cráft: to knów the fálse.

The one slightly puzzling line is the third, where we have the choice of putting our main sense stresses, therefore our metrical stresses, either on 'bore' and 'bairn', on 'bore' and 'blissful' or, as I have chosen to do, on 'blissful' and 'bairn'. None of these

three choices could be judged wrong: I base mine on the idea that
it is the blissfulness of the bairn and the fact that it is a bairn
that our thoughts are concentrated on, whereas the fact that Mary
bore it we are taking for granted. Two other readings strike me
as possible, but not like natural speech. The one reading which
would be both unlike natural speech and metrically impossible
would be:

> That bóre that blíssful báirn . . .

The half-line cannot have more than two stresses. But pure
stress verse of the Langland type, and of the type used in T. S.
Eliot's verse plays, differs from stress-syllable verse in that,
though there can never be any ambiguity about the number of main
stresses in a half-line, there can sometimes be a certain flexibility
about which these are. Langland could have written for instance:

> And bóre that heavenly báirn . . .

or

> That bóre that blíssful child . . .

or

> That sucked that blíssful báirn . . .

and in any of these three cases given us a metrically more satis-
factory half-line. But in each of these cases, as in the case of the
half-line he actually wrote, the sense-stress rhythm of the line is
that of natural speech or informal prose. The half-line is made
verse by the alliterative linkage with the first stressed syllable of
the second half-line. Each line divides into two equal halves, with
a sharp, abrupt and metrically necessary pause between them: and
each half-line has two stresses, stresses on the words (or on the
syllable of primary stress of words of more than one syllable)
that *mean* most in the context.

Since speech stress and verse stress completely coincide in pure stress verse, we need technical devices, like the sharp line break and the alliterative link (though we shall see that other devices are possible) to assure us that we are not reading prose. It should be noticed also that the *order* of words in Langland's passage is a completely natural speech order.

Pure stress metre is natural to our language. Small children writing poems, unless they have been encouraged to imitate rhymed stress-syllable stanzas, tend to write in short two-stress lines of pure stress verse, each line corresponding to a phrase, a clause or a short sentence; in other words to a unit of sense or meaning. We should not have learned to write stress-syllable, or accentual foot metre, except that poets like Chaucer borrowed syllable-count metres, with rhyme of eight and ten syllables, from French and found a foot pattern imposing itself, because of the importance of stress alternations in our language. Moreover, stress rhythm has never died out. It is the metre not only of old English poetry and of medieval alliterative poetry but of many nursery rhymes and playground dance games: of Skelton, at least when he is writing Skeltonics: of Hopkins, in his poems in 'sprung rhythm': of Eliot in much of his poetry from *Ash Wednesday* onwards, and in his verse plays with modern settings: of Auden, in a long and ambitious poem, *The Age of Anxiety*.

Nevertheless, since the early Renaissance, or indeed since Chaucer, most of our greatest poetry has been written not in pure stress verse but in stress-syllable verse. Pure stress verse is in a sense too easy to write: Robert Frost's quip about writing in free verse being like playing tennis without a net might more appropriately have been directed against pure stress verse (and much free verse, as we shall see later, can be seen as a more or less disguised form of pure stress verse). Any English passage of prose, for instance, can be broken, almost mechanically, into stress units, and into four-stress lines. Here is a fine passage by

Christopher Isherwood about revisiting England after the Second World War:

> Here was the scenery of the war – but already it was falling into disuse. Weeds were growing from the cracks in the concrete runway: the Army signposts and the camouflage on the hangars were weather-beaten and faded. Some Germans were strolling around with spades on their shoulders – no longer with the air of prisoners but of accepted inhabitants.

We can do this into neo-Langlandese quite easily:

> Hére wás
> The scénery of wár: – but alréady it was fálling
> Into disúse. Weéds were: grówing from the crácks
> In the cóncrete rúnways: the Ármy sígnposts
> And the cámouflágе on the hángars: were wéather-beaten and fáded.
> Sóme Gérmans: were strólling aróund
> With spádes on their shóulders: no lónger with the aír
> Of prísoners but óf: accépted inhábitants.

In the last line, I might have chosen instead to scan:

> Of prísoners bút of: accépted inhábitants,

or

> Of prísoners bút: of accépted inhábitants.

Isherwood's prose here is exceedingly concrete and poetic, and it would be rather pointless, for instance, to similarly transcribe into stress verse the abstract, expository sentences of this book. My point is that even without alliterative linkage the lines I have carved out of Isherwood are as clearly metrical as, for instance, the lines of Eliot's verse plays.

The nearness to prose of pure stress rhythm might well put

poets against it. But a poet can sometimes *want* a prosaic, or even a prosy, effect in verse. T. S. Eliot in *The Family Reunion, The Cocktail Party, The Confidential Clerk* and *The Elder Statesman* wanted to distract his readers, and even more his audiences, from a too acute consciousness of the fact that these plays are written in verse. Verse, even the verse of Shakespeare, has an effect for the modern audience of making the action taking place on the stage seem distant and artificial. At the same time, he wanted to slow down the delivery of speech, and to make his audiences more aware of the emotional implications of speech patterns than a prose dramatist usually can. He invented what he himself called a three-stress line, with two stresses on one side of a break in the middle, and one stress on the other (it did not matter to him on which side the one stress, and on which side the two stresses came). The stresses are sense stresses like those of the Langland line. I think myself that what he was using *was* the Langland line, that there are four sense-stresses, not three. But of four sense stresses in this kind of unit, one is often (in Langland also, for that matter) slightly less emphatic than the other three. I shall mark, in the following passage, the slightly less emphatic sense stress with a reversed stress mark, ` , so that the reader will see how Eliot is able to get only three main stresses, and I can find four, in his dramatic verse-line:

> It's Jóhn has had the áccident,: Làdy Monchénsey,
> And Wínchell télls me: Dr Ówen has sèen him
> And sáys it's nóthing: but a slìght concússion
> But he mustn't be móved toníght.: I'd trúst Òwen
> On a mátter like thís. You can trùst Ówen . . .

Eliot's conscious animadversion to only three stresses, his treatment of the fourth stress as secondary, enables the actors to ring the changes effectively on 'trúst Òwen' and 'trùst Ówen': but I would say that the fourth stress, the reversed one, is an integral part of the metre, though it is probably helpful for this kind of dramatic verse to mark the fourth stress *as* reversed.

Pure stress verse need not, however, be prosy. The beautiful invocation to the Lady in Eliot's *Ash Wednesday*, in short two-stress lines, shows a very different use of the medium:

> Lády of sílences
> Cálm and distréssed
> Tórn and most whóle
> Róse of mémory
> Róse of forgétfulness
> Exháusted and lífe-giving
> Wórried repóseful
> The síngle Róse
> Is nów the Gárden
> Where áll loves énd . . .

And if Langland's diction, like Eliot's in his later verse plays, is a very plain one, verging on the prosy, Anglo-Saxon verse had not only a stricter set of rules about stress combinations than Langland's but an extremely artificial diction, full of riddling peri-phrases or 'kennings' for everyday things, which perhaps had the function, since the basic rhythms were so similar, of emphasizing the distinction of verse from prose. In *The Age of Anxiety*, a long moral allegory or fable in alliterative pure stress verse, W. H. Auden, at the opposite extreme from Eliot in his verse plays, wishes to draw attention to the fact that he is writing verse, and his diction is therefore deliberately ornate, far-fetched, and full of kennings. It should be noticed, however, that (apart from object before subject in the first line) the word order is still more or less that of normal speech: for if we are puzzled about the sense, as I have noted already, we cannot get the stresses of pure stress verse right:

> All *w*ár's *w*óes: I can *w*éll imágine.
> *G*ún-barrels *g*línt,: *g*áthered in ámbush,

*M*áyhem among *m*óuntains; : *m*ínerals bréak
*Í*n by *ó*rder : on *í*ntimate gróups of
*T*énder *t*íssues; : at their toúgh vísit
*Fl*ésh *fl*ústers that was : so *fl*úent till nów,
*St*ámmers some nónsense, : *st*óps and *s*íts down,
Apa*th*étic to all *th*ís. : *Th*óusands líe in . . .

I am not sure about the scansion of the second last line, which reverses the usual pattern of two alliterative units in the first half and one in the second. A possible alternative scansion might be

*St*ámmers *s*óme nonsense, : *st*óps and sits dówn,

but then one wonders what is the sense justification for the stress on 'some' and is distracted by the two 's, t' combinations in the second half of the line. On the other hand, if 'sits' is intended to alliterate in a slightly irregular way, with the *t* in a forward rather than an initial position, the stress 'síts dòwn' seems slightly unnatural compared to the usual 'sìts dówn'. Perhaps the answer is that it is just not a very good line.

But let us see, now, what happens when pure stress metre is combined with rhyme. This happened first, significantly, in the work of the poet Skelton, who flourished in the earlier part of the reign of Henry VIII. Throughout the fifteenth century, stress-syllable metre, in the tradition of Chaucer, seemed to be breaking down in England. Various reasons are given for this fact. Though poets in the Chaucerian tradition were writing in stress-syllable metre, they did not *know* they were doing this – metrical theory follows very slowly indeed on the heels of metrical practice – and when they checked their lines for regularity must have done so mainly by counting syllables. But what was a syllable? The sounded final *e*, as in Chaucer's

Whán thǎt/Ǎpríl/lě wíth/ hǐs shóur/ěs sót (ě)

was still counted in scansion, but ceasing to be pronounced in ordinary speech. In words of French origin, like 'géntílésse' and 'cóurtĕsỳe' the French accent was moving back in the word and the word might also be taking a more English form: 'géntlĕnèss', 'cóurtĕsŷ'. Many traditional rhymes, however, implied the old pronunciation. A poet who is uncertain about the stresses of many of the key words he uses is in an unhappy position. Whatever the reason, many fifteenth-century English poets, like Stephen Hawes, seem to be writing syllabic verse in the sense they can count ten syllables, but are largely in the dark about where their stresses should come. (In Scotland, the language was not changing so rapidly; and the late fifteenth and very early sixteenth century, one of the weakest and most depressing periods in the history of English poetry, is the period, in Henryson, Dunbar, and Gawain Douglas, of the flowering of the Scottish medieval poetic tradition. These Scotsmen were great poets because, or partly because, unlike their English contemporaries, they had still a perfectly firm sense of how they wanted their lines to move.)

Skelton comes at the end of this depressing period and his reaction to it, in his best and most characteristic poems, is to give up the attempt to write stress-syllable verse. He restored a rough vigour to the debilitated poetry of the English fifteenth century by counting his sense stresses, ignoring the number of syllables of minor stress, and linking his short two-stress lines (the equivalent of Langland's half-line) by end-rhyme instead of by initial alliteration. Probably he did not consciously count his stresses. Uncertainty about what he is doing, or about whether he is writing proper verse at all, leads him to hammer away on one rhyme as long as possible, so as to keep up the linkage:

> But enfórsed am Í
> Ópenly to ascrý
> And to máke an outcrý
> Against ódious Envý,
> That évermore will lý
> And sáy cursedlý;

> With his lédder éy,
> And chékes drý;
> With viságe wán,
> As swárte as tán;
> His bónes cráke,
> His gúmmes rústy
> Are full únlústy . . .

One thing that should be noted is that this scans, in its simple way, whether Skelton or we say 'chekës' or 'cheeks', 'gummës' or 'gums' and whether we pronounce 'viságe' in the French way I have suggested by my scansion, or in the modern way, 'vísage'. The effect is of comic improvisation, of a metre just sustained by a sort of impudence: here and there I think Skelton distorts the pronunciation of common words to keep his rhymes going, as in 'cursedlý' instead of 'cúrsedly'.

Skelton, though famous, had very little direct effect on poetry in his own time. His successors in the later part of Henry VIII's reign were Wyatt and Surrey, much more subtle poets than he, but often very difficult to scan because often they did not know exactly what they were doing; but Surrey, the less interesting of the two, did rediscover the regular iambic line and also invented blank verse. The rediscovery of the regular iambic line hypnotized the early Elizabethan poets. George Gascoigne, who lived a most interesting life as a soldier of fortune and was one of the earliest professional English men of letters, wrote a pioneer short treatise on metrics in which he discovered that the iambic line is not only a line of ten syllables but of five alternating strong stresses. Unfortunately he and most of his immediate contemporaries thought the strong stresses had to be *very* strong, and that the safest way of keeping them right was by sticking as far as possible to monosyllabic words in poetry. It was not till the late 1580s that Sir Philip Sidney (who also introduced the trochaic metre into English lyrics, and introduced many new stanza forms from Italian and Spanish) gave the revived iambic line real life and flexibility.

Skelton, therefore, remained for a long time largely an historical curiosity. But one of the best poets of our own century, Robert Graves, very much admires him, and in one of his most beautiful early poems seems, at first sight, to be imitating him directly:

> Hé, of his géntlenèss,
> Thírsting and húngering,
> Wálked in the wíldernèss;
> Sóft words of gráce he spòke
> Únto lost désert-fòlk
> Thát listened wónderìng.
> He heárd the bíttern càll
> Fróm ruined pálace-wàll,
> Ánswered him brótherly;
> He héld commúnïon
> Wíth the she-pélican
> Óf lonely píety . . .

If we have just been reading Skelton, we shall read this passage of Graves in this way, as two stress lines with rhymes, often not only *rimes riches* but rhymes on syllables of minor stress. Yet it is a much more beautifully modulated passage than Skelton generally aims for or achieves, and we suddenly see that we can *also* scan it as a perfectly regular stress-syllable metre, dactylic dimeters – or lines of two feet, each foot marked thus ′ ° °. (*Dactyl* comes from the Greek word for finger: and our fingers have one long bone and two short.) Feet like the dactyl and the trochee ′ °, which start with the syllable of stronger stress, are sometimes described as falling feet, while feet like the iambus ° ′ and the anapaest ° ° ′, which start with the syllable or syllables of less stress are sometimes called rising feet. If we rescan Graves's passage in dactylics, we get this:

> Hé, òf hìs/ géntlènèss,
> Thírstìng aǹd/ húngèrìng

Wálked ĭn thĕ/ wíldĕrnĕss;
Sóft wŏrds ŏf/ gráce hĕ spŏke
Úntŏ lŏst / désĕrt-fŏlk
Thát lĭstĕnĕd / wóndĕrĭng.
Hé heărd thĕ / bíttĕrn căll
Fróm rŭĭned / pálăce-wăll,
Ánswĕrĕd hĭm / bróthĕrlў;
Hé hĕld cŏm/ mún–ĭ–ŏn
Wíth thĕ shĕ-/ pélĭcăn
Óf lŏnelў/ píĕtў . . .

Clearly, if we had not Skelton in mind, we would not be able
to read this passage aloud properly, with its unstressed rhymes,
and its medieval four-syllable pronunciation of 'communion'.
But clearly also, if we did not subconsciously recognize that it
was in very regular dactylics, we would not be able to give opening
syllables of the first dactyl as in 'Únto', 'Thát,' 'Hé' several times,
'Fróm', 'Wíth', and 'Óf' the strong metrical stress which is rarely
applied to pronouns and prepositions without a strong justification from an unusual sense-stress; though it might be said here
that the dactyls *impose* an unusual sense-stress, on the He (Christ)
as protagonist of the poem and on the prepositions as expressing
Christ's direct relationships with the creatures of the Wilderness.
This example is an important one, as showing how difficult it is
to be dogmatic about the scanning of a really interesting piece of
versification.

Such an ambivalence between pure stress versification and stress-
syllable versification is often a mark of the most interesting modern
poetry. Wimsatt has pointed out that the first few lines of the
fifth section of *The Waste Land*, the section called 'What the
Thunder Said', can be scanned as pure stress metrics:

Áfter the tórchlight : réd on swéaty faces
Áfter the frósty : sílence in the gárdens
Áfter the ágony : in stóny pláces

The shóuting and the crýing
Príson and pálace : and revérberátion . . .

They can also be scanned as very regular iambics:

Áftĕr/ thĕ tórch/ lĭght réd/ ŏn swéat/ ў́ fác(es)
Áftĕr/ thĕ fróst/ ў́ síl/ĕñce ín/ thĕ gárd(ens)
Áftĕr/ thĕ ág/ ŏný/ iñ stón/ ў́ plác(es)
Thĕ shóut/ ĭng ánd/ thĕ crý (ing)
Prísŏn/ ånd pál/åce ánd/ rĕvér/ bĕrá(tion)

Here, as in the Graves example, we perhaps need both of the
alternative scansions. In its simplicity, the pure stress scansion
suggests the emotional sweep, the primitive depth, of the passage;
in its hidden regularity, commanding every syllable, the stress-
syllable scansion suggests the icy control being exercised by the
poet's making mind. Both scansions are correct; to see the validity
of both of them, as W. K. Wimsatt does, is brilliant.

The great modern innovator in pure stress verse was, of course,
Gerard Manley Hopkins, though his own metrical theories are
sometimes, in his expression of them, difficult to understand.
Though he insisted on his verses in 'sprung rhythm' being
scanned on the stress, he also thought of them as composed of
feet, which could have a varying number of unstressed syllables
or syllables of minor stress coming after the main stress. A 'foot'
in this sense could be as long as five syllables or as short as one.

This free handling of the foot, even when combined with an
overmastering attention to stress, gave Hopkins 'the roll, the
rise, the carol, the creation' which we do not find, for instance,
in Langland, in Skeltonica, in Eliot's verse plays or in Auden's
The Age of Anxiety.

3
Stress – Syllable Metres

Most of the greatest and most ambitious English poetry is written
in a five stress line of, at its most regular, ten syllables, which can be
divided into five feet in which the syllable of minor stress precedes
the syllable of greater stress. The most common name for this
line is the iambic pentameter. It need not be a line of merely ten
syllables. If it has a weak or feminine ending, but is otherwise
regular, it is a line of eleven syllables like

1　2　3　4　5　6　7　8　9　10　11
I come to bury Caesar not to praise him

It is possible to substitute in some feet, though not in too many,
a three syllable foot for a two syllable foot, and this license occurs
even in very regular early blank verse:

Måde gló / rǐoůs súm/měr bỳ / thǐs sún/ǒf Yórk

The two final syllables of 'glorious', in the line from *Richard III*
quoted above, could be considered as contracted into something
like 'gloryous', and in the printed texts of poets of the sixteenth
and seventeenth century there are often marks of elision that
suggest they felt uneasy about having three syllable feet. But by
the early eighteenth century, what Pope thought (rightly to my
mind) his most melodious line has no elision in the foot that gives
the line its peculiar melody:

See where/ Maeot/is sleeps/ and hard/ly flows
Thě fréez/iňg Tán/åǐs thróugh/ å wáste/ ǒf snóws.

A reader who ignorantly pronounced, or contracted, 'Tanais' to 'Tana's' or 'Tan'is' would utterly destroy the beauty of this line. These three syllable feet in iambic lines are sometimes called anapaestic substitutions. They scan in the same way as the anapaestic foot, a three syllable rising foot which is scanned thus ° ° ′. But proper anapaests move at a kind of coarse gallop, as in Byron's

Thĕ Ăssýr/ iăn cǎme dówn/ lĭke ă wólf/ ŏn thĕ fóld,

whereas Pope's trisyllabic foot '-aĭs thróugh' helps to slow down the line. Trisyllabic substitution is therefore a better term than anapaestic substitution. These trisyllabic substitutions can occur anywhere in the line but since properly anapaestic lines often include some iambic feet, a line with three or four trisyllabic substitutions would tend to appear basically anapaestic. The anapaestic line, as well as being useful for rough, galloping verse like Byron's poem about the Assyrians, lends itself admirably to comic verse. In reading eighteenth-century couplets, of a comic or satirical sort, it is important to distinguish between the heroic couplet proper, in iambics, like Pope's:

Nóthĭng/ mŏre trúe/ thăn whát/ yóu ŏnce/ lĕt fáll:
'Móst wŏm/ ĕn háve/ nŏ chár/ ăctérs/ ăt áll',

and the comic anapaestic tetrameter couplet like Goldsmith's:

Herĕ líes/ Dăvĭd Gárr/ĭck, dĕscríbe/ hĭm whŏ cán,
Ăn ăbrídge/ mĕnt ŏf áll/ thăt ĭs pléas/ănt ĭn mán.

It should be noticed that one iambic foot there does not rob the first line of its basically anapaestic character, any more than one or two trisyllabic substitutions rob an iambic line of its basically iambic character. But it should be noticed that where trisyllabic substitutions in iambic lines are usually intended to achieve some special aesthetic effect, iambic substitutions in anapaestic verse are due to the difficulty of finding a succession of purely anapaestic feet in English.

Iambic verse lends itself to serious and reflective poetry better than anapaestic verse partly because there is a strong iambic element in ordinary English speech rhythm. Anapaestic rhythms do not occur continuously in ordinary English speech, so the most skilful poem in anapaests will tend to have a feeling of contrivance, of the 'false gallop of verse'.

The other important kind of substitution of foot in the iambic line is what is sometimes called reversal of the iambic foot and sometimes trochaic substitution: the substitution of ′ ° for ° ′. Not everybody would agree with my scanning of the first line of Pope's 'Characters of Women':

Nóthĭng/ mŏre trúe/ thăn whát/ yóu ŏnce/ lĕt fáll,

and, of course, the alternative scansion 'yŏu ónce' is perfectly possible. I think Pope would have us stress 'you' because he is paying an arch compliment to the penetration of Martha Blount, to whom he is addressing the epistle. If we accept my scansion, it is clear that reversal of the foot, or trochaic substitution, in the second last (or penultimate) foot does not at all affect the regularity of the line. Reversal or trochaic substitution on the second foot is, however, very unusual, so that Palgrave in *The Golden Treasury* called special attention to this line of Shelley's

Ănd wíld / rósĕs/ ănd ív/ ў̆ sérp/ ĕntíne . . .

where almost any other poet would have written

Ănd rós/ ĕs wíld/ ănd ív/ ў̆ sérp/ ĕntíne . . .

In great passages of verse, however, the iambic line makes its effect not in isolation but as part of a verse paragraph. The two English poets whom it is most interesting to contrast from this point of view are Shakespeare, as the master of the dramatic verse paragraph, and Milton, as the master of the epic verse paragraph. Very different as Shakespeare and Milton are, they both feel that in verse that aims at great dignity rhyme must be dispensed with. In a poem that is neither epical nor dramatic, but that follows a complex thought movement, like Wordsworth's *The Prelude*, rhyme is also felt to be out of place. Hearing such poems read aloud, we have no doubt at all that we are listening to poetry, but we might often be uncertain (particularly when the sense is run on from line to line, without punctuational pauses at the end of the line) how the lines divide. This is what Dr Johnson meant when he said that English blank verse is often only verse to the eye.

Here, for instance, is a passage from Milton's *Paradise Lost*, the ninth book, picked at random:

> Such pleasure took the Serpent to behold
> This flowery plat, the sweet recess of Eve
> Thus early, thus alone; her heavenly form
> Angelic, but more soft and feminine,
> Her gracious innocence, her every air
> Of gesture or least action, overawed
> His malice, and with rapine sweet bereaved
> His fierceness of the fierce intent it brought.

We can imagine somebody hearing this passage, taking it down in shorthand, knowing it was in iambic lines, and dividing it, not implausibly, thus:

> Such pleasure took
> The Serpent to behold this flowery plat,
> The sweet recess of Eve thus early, thus
> Alone; her heavenly form angelic, but
> More soft and feminine, her gracious innocence,
> Her every air of gesture or least action,
> Overawed his malice and with rapine sweet
> Bereaved his fierceness of the fierce intent
> It brought . . .

One line in this redivision is an Alexandrine, or six-foot line:

> Môre sóft/ aňd fém/iňíne,/ hěr grác/ioǔs ín/nôcénce

Yet, on the whole, Milton's 'linked harmony' is preserved. It is probable, then, that for the listening ear the music of such verse is not in the individual line but in the verse paragraph and its subtle modulations.

It should be noted (I shall scan the lines in Milton's own division of them) that the sense of subtle modulation in this passage does not depend on any use of substitution or reversal. The lines are extremely regular:

> Sǔch pléas/ ǔre tóok/ thě Sérp/eňt tó/ běhóld
> Thǐs flów/ erỳ plát,/ thě swéet/ rěcéss/ ôf Éve
> Thǔs eár/lỳ thús/ ǎlóne;/ hěr héaven/lỳ fórm
> Aňgél/ič, bút/ môre sóft/ aňd fém/ iníne.
> Hěr grác/ ioǔs ínn/océncé,/ hěr év/erỳ aír
> Ôf gést/ǔre ór/leǎst áct/iǒn óv/ ěráwed
> Hǐs mál/iče, ánd/wǐth ráp/iňe swéet/ běreáved
> Hǐs fiérce/něss óf/ thě fiérce/ǐntént/ǐt bróught.

The regularity gives an effect of what seventeenth-century critics called smoothness or sweetness, which is appropriate to the beauty and charm of Eve. In dealing with grimmer topics, Milton can be much more rugged, as in the line:

> Fallen Cherub, to be weak is miserable,

but he aimed on the whole, for the sake of the dignity of epic poetry, at regularity and is, if one allows for changed pronuncia-

tions and occasional very heavy iambic feet like 'Rocks, fens . . .' much more regular, much more easily scanned, than is generally supposed.

Shakespeare is different. Dramatic blank verse had to sound like speech. Shakespeare started as an imitator of Marlowe, writing it, and thinking it out, in single well balanced lines, none of which (even if there is no punctuation mark at the end of the line) really runs into the next, each of which is a self-contained unit, and all of which are cast in a remarkably similar mould:

> Nów ĭs/ thĕ wínt/ĕr óf/ oŭr dís/ cŏntént
> Măde glór/ioŭs súm/ mĕr bý/ thĭs sún/ ŏf Yórk
> Ănd áll/thĕ clóuds/ thăt loúred/ ŭpón/ oŭr hóuse
> Ín thĕ / deĕp bós/ ŏm óf/ thĕ Óc/ĕan búr(ied).

The last line of course becomes more interesting metrically if one reflects that 'Ocean' was often pronounced 'Ocëan' and that 'buried' could be 'burièd': we could then get an Alexandrine, and one that, to my ear, is very pleasing:

> Ín thĕ/deĕp bós/ ŏm óf/ thĕ Óc/ĕan búr/iĕd.

But on the whole these early lines have a mechanical regularity; they are easy not only to scan but to write, and John Barton, in his recension of the three parts of Henry VI into two plays at Stratford, was able to add quite long passages of his own that were indistinguishable, metrically and in their general rhetorical pattern, from the Bard's own work.

My rearrangement of the Milton passage about Eve had more run on lines than Milton had and produced, perhaps, a certain slight effect of informality and breathlessness, not really suitable for epic poetry, but very suitable for dramatic verse. If we move on from Shakespeare's earliest style we shall find a similar informality and breathlessness in Hamlet's speech about Rosencrantz and Guildenstern's plot against him, and his detection of it. T. S. Eliot described this passage as typical of Shakespeare's 'most mature' blank verse.

> Úp frŏm/ mў cáb(in)
> Mў séa- /gŏwn scárf'd/ ăboút/ mĕ, ín/ thĕ dárk
> Gròped Í/ tŏ fínd /oùt thém; / hád mў/ dĕsíre,
> Fíngĕr'd/ thĕir páck/ĕt, ánd/ ĭn fíne/ wĭthdréw
> Tŏ míne/ òwn róom /ăgáin;/ mákĭng/ sò bóld,
> Mў féars/ fŏrgétt/ ĭng mánn/ ĕrs, tŏ/ ŭnséal

Thĕir gránd/ cŏmmíss/iŏn; whére/ Ĭ fóund/ Hŏrá(tio),
Ò róy/ ăl knáv/ ĕrŷ! – ăn ĕxáct/ cŏmmánd,
Lárdĕd/ wĭth mán/ ŷ díff/ ĕrĕnt/ sórts / ŏf réas(ons),
Ĭmpórt/ ĭṅg Dén/ màrk's héalth,/ aṅd Éng/ laṅd's tóo,
Wĭth hó!/ sùch búgs/ aṅd gób/lĭns ĭn/ mỳ lífe,
Thát, ŏn/ thĕ súp/ ĕrvíse,/ nŏ léis/urĕ bát(ed),
Nò, nót/ tŏ stáy/ thĕ grínd/ĭṅg óf /thĕ áxe,
My héad/ shŏuld bé/ strùck óff.

If we compare this passage with the Milton passage we shall note
the number of reversed feet, particularly in the fourth place,
'hád mỳ/ dĕsíre', 'máking/ sò bóld', and the number of feet like
'Gròped Ĭ', 'sò bóld', in which both syllables are strongish, and in
which a good actor might well wish to say: 'Gróped Ĭ' or 'só
bòld'.

Before leaving the iambic pentameter line, I should note that
it is my experience that students who recognize this line immediately in Shakespeare, Milton and Wordsworth often assume that
modern poets writing in iambic pentameters are writing in a sort
of free verse: two great modern American poets, about whom I
have found this mistake frequently made, are Wallace Stevens
and Robert Frost. I end this section with sample scansions of
two short passages, the first by Stevens, one of the great masters
of meditative blank verse in our century, the second by Frost,
one of the great masters of conversational blank verse. Here is the
wonderful last stanza of Stevens' poem 'Sunday Morning'. I have
marked the last two feet of the first line of this passage as a pyrrhic
succeeded by a spondee, in spite of the Trager-Smith doctrine,
to which I have alluded, that this succession is impossible in
English accentual verse: it also occurs elsewhere:

Shĕ héars,/ ŭpón/ thăt wát/ ĕr wĭth /oút soúnd,
Ă voíce/ thăt críes,/ 'Thĕ tómb /ĭn Pál /ĕstíne
Ĭs nót/ thĕ pórch / ŏf spír / ĭts líng / ĕríng.

Ĭt ís/ thĕ gráve/ ŏf Jés/ ŭs whére/ hĕ láy.'
Wĕ líve/ ĭn ăn /óld chá/ ŏs óf/ thĕ sún,
Ŏr óld/ dĕpénd/ ĕncў/ ŏf dáy/ ănd níght,
Ŏr ísl/ ănd sól/ ĭtúde,/ ŭnspóns/ ŏred, frée,
Ŏf thát/ wĭde wát/ ĕr, ín/ ĕscáp/ ăblĕ,
Deèr wálk/ ŭpón/ oŭr móun/ taĭns, ănd/ thĕ quáil
Whístlĕ/ ăbóut /ŭs /théir/ spŏntán/eŏus críes;
Swèet bérr/ iĕs ríp/ ĕn ín/ thĕ wíld/ ĕrnèss;
Ánd, ĭn/ thĕ ís/ŏlá/tiŏn ôf/ thĕ sk‎ý
Ăt éve/ nĭng cás/ ŭăl flócks/ ŏf píg/eŏns máke
Ămbíg/ ŭoŭs únd/ ŭlát/iŏns âs / thĕy sínk,
Dównwărd/ tŏ dárk/ nĕss, ŏn/ĕxténd/ ĕd wíngs.

The extremely calm regularity of the movement of this passage
is notable, there is a kind of quiet lulling, lapping noise, which
one seems to associate with the frequent images of water, and
perhaps with the repeated initial *w*'s 'wide water', 'whistle',
'wilderness', and the final 'wings'. The effect is meditative and
lyrical and we do not at first notice that we are reading blank
verse. There are many echoic effects, vowel variations and
exploitation to quantity.

The following passage is from Frost's 'The Death of the Hired
Man', a great pastoral poem in a tradition of realistic pastoral
deriving from both Wordsworth and Crabbe. Though the first
lines of most poems tend to be very regular, the first line of this
is very hard to scan, and reads like prose; and Frost's consciousness
of speech rhythm is so much more obvious than his underlying
metrical regularity that one understands why young readers
sometimes take him to be writing free verse.

Márȳ/ săt mús/ĭng ŏn/ thĕ lámp-/fláme ăt/ thĕ táb(le)
Waítĭng/ fŏr Wár/ rĕn. Whèn/ shĕ heárd/ hĭs stép,
Shĕ rán/ ŏn típ-/ tŏe dówn/ thĕ dárk/ĕned páss(age)
Tŏ méet/ hĭm ĭn/ thĕ doór/ wăy wĭth/ thĕ néws
Ănd pút/ hĭm ŏn/ hĭs guárd. /'Sílăs/ ĭs báck.'

Shĕ púshed/ hĭm oút/ wărd wíth/ hĕr thróugh/thĕ dóor
Ănd shút/ ĭt áft/ ĕr hĕr./ 'Bĕ kínd,'/ shĕ sáid.
Shĕ toók/ thĕ márk/ ĕt thíngs/ frŏm Wár/rĕn's árms
Ănd sét/ thĕm ôn/ thĕ pórch,/ thĕn dréw/ hĭm dówn
Tŏ sít/ bĕsíde/ hĕr ôn/ thĕ wóod/ ĕn stéps.

The frequent weak feet here, 'hĭm în', 'hĭm ôn', 'thĕm ôn', and
so on, are not attempts at accentual pyrrhics, like the two weak
feet in the Stevens' passage, but simply faithful reflections of
conversational sentence stress. The first line could be the opening
sentence of a prose story, and to scan it at all seems slightly artificial. There is nothing of Stevens' attention to echoic effects,
vowel variation, quantity: all the more seductive qualities of
versification are sacrificed as it were to preserving the stresses,
intonations, syntax of natural speech. But there are one or two
strictly regular lines like

Shĕ púshed/ hĭm oút/wărd wíth/ hĕr thróugh/ thĕ dóor,

where the little word 'with', weak in itself, rightly gets a strong
stress for sense, to remind us that it is verse not prose that we are
reading. Ezra Pound and other experimenters have spoken a great
deal about poets in this century 'breaking the tyranny of the
iambic line'. These two passages, utterly different in tone and
movement, may remind us both what an extraordinarily flexible
instrument the iambic pentameter is, and also that much of
the greatest modern poetry is written in this line, and not in free
verse.

IAMBIC TETRAMETERS, TRIMETERS AND LONGER
IAMBIC LINES

Shorter types of iambic line raise interesting metrical problems,
but not of the same type as the iambic tetrameter. The possibility
of foot reversal, or trochaic substitution, makes it sometimes hard

to tell whether a poem in tetrameters is fundamentally iambic or trochaic:

> Úndĕr / néath thĭs / sáblĕ/ heárse
> Liés thĕ / súbjĕct/ ŏf áll/ vérse:
> Sídneў's/ sístĕr,/ Pémbrŏke's/ móthĕr.
> Deáth, ĕre/ thóu tăke/ súch ăn/ óthĕr
> Faír ănd / wíse ănd/ goód ăs/ shé,
> Tíme shăll/ thrów ă/ dárt ăt/ thée.

This famous epigram is clearly trochaic, with the last trochee in some lines truncated. But what of Shakespeare's 'The Phoenix and the Turtle'? When we scan trochaically

> Lét thĕ / bírd ŏf / loúdĕst/ láy
> Ón thĕ/ sóle Ăr/ ábiăn/ trée
> Hérăld/ sád ănd/ trúmpĕt/ bé,

we feel instinctively that this misrepresents the movement of the lines, which is better represented thus:

> Lét/ thĕ bírd/ ŏf loúd/ ĕst láy
> Ón/ thĕ sóle/ Ăráb/ iăn trée
> Hér/ăld sád/ ănd trúmpĕt bé.

The tetrameter, a four beat line, can be of seven syllables as well as eight: as it can end with a shortened trochee, so it can begin with the stressed syllable of a shortened iambic foot. When we reflect on this, we may begin to wonder whether the little epigram on Sidney's sister *is* trochaic all through. The movement, certainly, of the first three lines is a heavily and dolefully falling movement. But might not the movement of the last three, with their rising and asserting note, be better represented by the scansion:

> Deáth,/ ĕre thóu/ tăke súch/ ănóth(er),
> Fáir/ ănd wíse/ ănd goód/ ăs shé,
> Tíme/ shăll thrów/ ă dárt/ ăt thée.

Our scansion of tetrameters, in other words, cannot be mechanical even to the degree that our scansion of the pentameter sometimes can be: it must depend very much on our sense of movement and phrasing.

Two poems which lend themselves excellently to exercises in the scanning of tetrameters are Milton's *L'Allegro* and *Il Penseroso*, which are basically iambic in movement, but with a good deal of trochaic substitution, and with many passages that lend themselves to dual scansion:

> Háste thêe,/ Nými, aṅd/ bríng wǐth/ thée
> Jést aṅd/ yóuthfǔl/ Jóllǐ/ tý . . .

> Háste/ thêe, Nými/ aṅd bríng/ wǐth thée
> Jést/ aṅd youth/ fǔl Jóll/ ǐtỹ . . .

In our own age, one of the poets who has made a really interesting and novel use of the shorter iambic lines is W. B. Yeats. I have heard a good critic, the late Douglas Browne, describe one of his greatest poems, 'Easter 1916', as written in iambic tetrameters. To my ear it is clearly written in a line which, in his specially flexible use of it, can be considered almost as Yeats's own invention: an iambic trimeter, or three-foot line, with very free trisyllabic substitution and occasional very daring reversal. Here is my scansion of the beginning of the poem:

> Iˮ hǎve mét/thêm ǎt clóse/ ôf dáy
> Cómiṅg/ wǐth vív/ ǐd fác(es)
> Frôm coúnt/êr ôr désk/ ǎmôṅg gréy
> Eíghteênth-/ cénturỹ/ hoúsês.
> Î hǎve pássed/wǐth ǎ nód/ ôf thê héad
> Ôr pôlité/ meáníṅg/ lêss wórds,
> Ôr havê líṅg/êred ǎwhíle/ aṅd saíd
> Pôlíte/ méaníṅg/ lêss wórds,

It may seem odd to describe a metre as basically iambic when on pure foot count, there are rather more three-syllable feet than two-syllable feet. The two-syllable foot nevertheless remains the norm and the trisyllabic substitutions are to relax it into a conversational tone. At solemn or high moments in the poem, the regular iambic trimeter reasserts itself:

> Whăt vóice / mŏre swéet/ thăn hérs
> Whĕn, yoúng / ănd beaú/ tĭfúl,
> Shĕ róde / tŏ hárr/ ĭérs?

This little book is intended to be suggestive rather than exhaustive, and iambic lines other than the pentameter, the tetrameter and the trimeter, particularly in Yeats's use of it, do not seem to me to present many puzzles. Of the longer lines, the Alexandrine, or six-foot iambic line, is useful to end a stanza with. Dryden liked to intersperse his heroic couplets with occasional Alexandrines, but Pope, a neater though not a greater poet, thought it a useless encumbrance:

> A needless Alexandrine ends the song,
>   That, like a wounded snake, drags its slow length along.

A whole poem written in Alexandrines would tire the ear, and this is even truer of the fourteener, which was very popular with Elizabethan poets of the drab period and was sometimes alternated with Alexandrines. Saintsbury quotes this example from Surrey:

> Goŏd lá/ diĕs, yé/ thăt háve/: yoŭr pleás/urĕs ín/ ĕxíle,
> Stĕp ín/ yoŭr foót,/ cŏme táke/ ă pláce/ ănd móurn/ wĭth mé/ ă whíle;
>   Ănd súch/ ăs bý/thĕir lords/: dŏ sét/ bŭt lít/tlĕ príce,
> Lĕt thém/ sĭt stíll,/ ĭt skílls/thĕm nót/ whăt chánce/ cŏme ón/ thĕ díce.

Saintsbury notes that there is very little to be said for these thumping lines except as 'a school of regular rhythm'. He notes that broken into 'short measure' (6, 6, 8, 6) it has not been ineffective in hymns. He might have noted that the fourteener by itself breaks into something more interesting – ballad metre (8, 6). Thus a fourteener of Surrey's broken down is in exactly the same metre, though not nearly as subtly handled, as the ballad of Sir Patrick Spens:

> Stĕp ín/ yŏur fóot,/ cŏme táke/ ă pláce,
> Ănd moúrn/ wĭth mé/ ă whíle . . .

> Thĕ Kíng/ síts ĭn/ Dùnférm/ lĭne toún
> Drínkĭng/ thĕ bloód-/ rĕd wíne . . .

The Scottish ballad is much more metrically interesting than the transformed Surrey line, simply because when we are composing in lines of eight and six syllables (in iambic tetrameters and trimeters) we feel free to reverse feet, whereas the fourteener, unwieldy thing that it is, can only remain recognizable as a line of verse by being monotonously and regularly iambic all through.

TROCHAIC, ANAPAESTIC, DACTYLIC AND CHORIAMBIC LINES

I have deliberately given the lion's share of this chapter to various types of iambic line, both because most of the greatest English poetry is written in iambic lines, and because iambic metres, on account of the licences of substitution and reversal, are more flexible and technically interesting than other English metres. Most of what needs to be said about trochaic metres has been said already in connection with the iambic tetrameter. Trochees lend themselves better, it can be additionally noted here, than iambics to a certain kind of singing effect in poetry (the iambic foot is eminently the *speaking* foot): a good example of their sweetness to the ear is the song that the boy sings to Mariana in Shakespeare's *Measure for Measure*:

> Táke, Ŏ/ táke thŏse/ líps ă / wáy,
> Thát sŏ/ sweétlў/ wére fŏr/ swórn;
> Ánd thŏse / eyés, thĕ / bréak ŏf / dáy,

Líghts thât / dó mîs/ leád thê/ mórn:
Bút mŷ/ kíssês bríng å/ gaín, (bríng å/gaín)
Seáls ôf / lóve, bût/ séaled iñ/ váin, (séaled în/ váin).

The repetitions of 'bring again' and 'sealed in vain' at the end of
the last two lines which I have bracketed off do not alter the
metre but are purely for the convenience of the composer of the
air and of the singer: the truncated final trochee is simply repeated
once, without, in its first occurrence, losing its character of
finality.

In contrasting iambic pentameter couplets with anapaestic
tetrameter couplets, we have already noted the galloping movement of the anapaest, and the fact that anapaestic feet lend themselves much less easily to natural speech rhythms than iambic feet.
In comic verse, therefore, like the following stanza from Winthrop
Mackworth Praed's 'A Letter of Advice', anapaestic lines permit
of a certain amount of iambic substitution to preserve a natural
tone:

Rêmém/ bêr thê thríll/ iñg rômánc(es)
    Wê reád/ oñ thê bánk / ôf thê glén;
Rêmém/ bêr the súit/ ôrs oûr fánc(ies)
    Woûld píc/tûre fôr bóth/ ôf ûs thén.
Thêy wóre/ thê rêd cróss/ oñ thêir shóuld(er),
    Theŷ hâd ván/ quîshed añd pár/doñed thêir foe —
Sweêt friénd, / arê yôu wís/ êr ôr cóld(er)?
    Mŷ ówn/ Ârâmin/tå, såy 'Nó!'

Notice that only one line, the third last, begins with an anapaestic
and not an iambic foot. In non-comic verse, iambic substitution is
less frequent.

The example of dactylic metre which we gave in comparing a
passage by Robert Graves with one by Skelton is probably as
effective an example of this metre, one not very natural or easy to
use in English stress-syllable verse, as one could find. Saintsbury

notes that a long line of Tennyson's is probably intended as an eight-foot line in dactylics:

Whén frŏm thĕ/ térrŏrs ŏf/ Nátŭre ă/ peóplĕ hăve/ fáshiŏñed
ańd/ wórshĭp ă/ spírĭt ŏf/ Évĭl,

but that it reads best as an anapaestic line with a push-off stressed syllable (technically called an anacrusis, in English sometimes a 'catch').

The following passage from Tennyson's *Maud* can, I think, be scanned plausibly as dactylic hexameters with some trochaic substitution. Here is my dactylic foot-division:

Cóld ańd cléar-cŭt / fáce, whŷ/ cóme yŏu sŏ/ crúĕllŷ/ méek,
Breákiñg ă/ slúmbĕr ĭn/ whích àll /spléenfŭl/ follŷ wăs/ drówned . . .

Tennyson, like most poets with a classical education, was very much aware of quantity even when writing stress-syllable verse. My scansion here is based on the conviction that the movement of these lines is basically a falling rather than a rising movement, and that the strong final syllables (which are also rhyming words) need isolation as the first, stressed syllables of uncompleted dactyls. Simpler examples of dactylic metre in shorter lines can be found in Victorian short poems, like Tom Hood's:

Óne mŏre ŭn/ fórtŭnăte,
Weárŷ ŏf/breáth,
Ráshlŷ ĭmp/ pórtŭnăte,
Góne tŏ hĕr/ deáth . . .

There is room in this chapter, I think, for consideration of one more metre: choriambics. A choriambic foot is composed of a trochee followed by an iambic foot, thus ′ ° ° ′, and lines written in choriambics have a pleasantly rocking, almost see-saw effect.

J. B. Leishman invents this strophe as an English equivalent of the Horatian choriambic strophe:

Bōrn whīle/ gōds wĕre bĕnīgn,/ gōds wĕre bĕnīgn/ tŏ āll,
bōrn whīle/gōds wĕre bĕnīgn/ gōds wĕre bĕnīgn/ tŏ āll,
  bōrn whīle/ gōds wĕre bĕnīgn/ ănt,
bōrn whīle/ gōds wĕre bĕnīgn/ tŏ āll.

It is his theory that all words or syllables that can take a main
sense stress in English can be counted as long, and those that can
take a minor stress can be counted as short. This theory is far
too simple, but Leishman's is the most intelligent recent discussion
of the possibility of writing quantitative verse in English, and
therefore his choriambics make a useful transition to our next,
chapter.

4
Quantitative Metres and Pure Syllabic Metres

QUANTITATIVE METRES

I am assuming in this chapter that the reader either knows no Latin or, like myself, learned some Latin at school but was never properly drilled in Latin metres. Spoken Latin had some stress, but nothing like the important phenomenon it is in English speech. Lines of Latin verse are made up of feet counted by the duration of syllables; thus the dactyl, ¯ ˘ ˘, is equivalent to the spondee, ¯ ¯, in the time it takes to pronounce. The length of a syllable, however, should not be confused, either in English or Latin, with the length of a vowel or diphthong.

Leishman, whose interesting book *Translating Horace* I am using as my point of departure in this chapter, felt that it would be quite easy to write English verse reproducing the patterns of Horatian strophes if we considered words in action, not in the dictionary, and realized that the same word can often be long by dictionary definition and short by rhetorical emphasis. He ignored the fact that in stress-syllable verse metrical stress cannot make a short syllable long, nor can lack of metrical stress make a long syllable short. He was essentially a classicist and where he can he likes to scan iambic pentameters quantitatively.

Leishman illustrates the scansion of the Horatian Alcaic stanza thus. I give the original Latin, and his own translation. He invented a special symbol, ᷤ to indicate that though a vowel was short a syllable was long, but in copying his scansion I have substituted the ordinary sign for a long syllable ¯. Attention to syllabic endings is more important in quantitative scansion than attention to the natural length or shortness of vowels taken in isolation. Here, then, are Horace's Latin and Leishman's English Alcaics:

> Ō/ dĭvă, / grātūm / / quāe rĕgĭs/ Āntĭ/ ŭm,
> prāe/sēns vĕ/l īmō/ / tōllĕrĕ/ dē gră/ dū
>   mōr/tālĕ/ cōrpūs/ vēl sŭ/pērbōs
>   vērtĕrĕ/ fūnĕrĭ/būs trĭ/ ūmphōs.

> Ō/ gōddĕss/ rūl*īng* / / fōrtŭnăte/ Āntĭ/ŭm,
> nōw/ mānĭ/fēst *in* / / rāisĭng frŏm/lōw dĕ/grēe
>   oūr/mōrtăl/ clāy, *ānd*/ nōw ĭn/ tūrnĭng
>   īnto ă/fūn'răl the/ prōudĕst/ trĭŭmph.

The first two lines of the strophe are Alcaic hendecasyllabics. They begin with a single long syllable, the anacrusis, 'catch', or push-off syllable. Leishman compares it to the striking of a note before the singing of an unaccompanied song. I have quoted already these two lines of an old Scottish ballad:

> The king sits in Dunfermline toun,
>   Drinking the blood-red wine . . .

We can imagine a singer rendering this:

> O, the king sits in Dunfermline toun
> A- drinking the blood-red wine . . .

The O and the A- there would be anacruses. In Horace, the anacrusis could be long, like the O there, or short like the A. In Horace it is mostly long. The anacrusis is followed by a trochee, and then by a spondee, and then by a strong breath-pause, or caesura, which like the middle break in Anglo-Saxon four-stress alliterative verse is an essential part of the metre, not, like the mobile and occasionally optional caesura in the iambic pentameter, something that belongs to the poem's general rhetoric, rather than specifically to the metre of the line. The caesura is followed by a dactyl, a trochee, and a detached final syllable which may be either long or short. The third line is a shorter, nine-syllable line, with no caesura: it consists of an anacrusis, a trochee, a spondee, another trochee, and may end either with a trochee or a spondee (in Horace it ends with a spondee, in Leishman with a trochee). The fourth line is of ten syllables, again has no caesura (and also no anacrusis or detached final syllable) and consists of two dactyls followed either by two trochees or a trochee and spondee.

Leishman himself has marked three syllables, the '-ing' of 'ruling', 'in' in the second line, and 'and' in the third, where he admits that the English reader might go astray, not lingering and pausing enough in the first two lines, not giving 'and' enough weight and length in the third line, unless he had already some notion of what sort of strophe he was meant to be reading. It seems to me that a reader used to English stress-syllable verse, and supposing this to be an example of it, would feel something slightly odd about the strophe but might well attempt to scan it like this:

> Ŏ gód/dĕss rúl/liñg fórt/ uñate Ánt/ĭúm
> nŏw mán/ĭfést/ iñ ráis/iñg frŏm lów/ dĕgrée
> oŭr mór/tăl cláy/ añd nów/iñ túrn(ing)
> íntŏ/ ă fún/ ĕrál/thĕ próud/es̆t trí(umph).

The quantitative stanza, worked on with such care by Leishman, becomes in fact two stress-syllable iambic pentameters, with the perfectly permissible licence of an anapaest or trisyllabic foot in the fourth place, the third line becomes a perfectly regular iambic tetrameter with a feminine ending, and the fourth an iambic pentameter regular but for the very common trochaic first foot, and with a feminine ending. Moreover, because our sense of stress difference in English is so much more alert than our sense of quantitative difference, it seems to me that it would be difficult even for Leishman himself to read the strophe aloud in a way that would not make the underlying stress-syllable iambic pattern, built into our language, more prominent to the ear than the quantitative differences. And this difficulty faces the most skilful poets.

I would like, however, to quote and scan some strophes from a poem by a very fine modern poet, Louis MacNeice, who taught Greek at one time first at Birmingham, then at Bedford College, London University. This is an example of Sapphics, another Horatian metre. The Sapphic stanza consists of a Sapphic hendeca-syllabic, a line of eleven syllables, thrice repeated, and followed by a line called an Adonic, consisting of a dactyl followed by a spondee or a trochee. The eleven-syllable line consists of a trochee followed by a spondee at the beginning, a dactyl inter-rupted by a strong caesura, and then at the end a trochee and spondee again. (There are thus five syllables in the first half of the line, six in the second.) But MacNeice does not put himself into a mechanical straitjacket. He allows himself lines of twelve or thirteen syllables, does not always try to impose a dactylic or trochaic downbeat on the natural iambic upbeat of English, perhaps expects us not to elide but to leave out of our scansion count certain small syllables. The result might be called free sapphics, but strangely it makes us much more aware of quantity, less inclined to impose a stress-syllable rhythm, than the more meticulously scholarly efforts of Leishman. Here are some strophes tentatively scanned:

Ōr bĕ/twēen bēech(es)/ vēr/ /dŭroŭs/ănd vŏl/ūpt(u)ōus
Ōr whĕre/ brōom ānd/ gōrse/ / bĕ/flāgged thĕ/chālklānd —
Āll thĕ/ flāre ānd/ gūst/ /ŏ ŏf th(e)/ūnĕn/dūrīng
     Jōys ŏf ă/ sēasŏn.

Īf ŏn(ly)/ yōu wōuld/ cōme/ / ănd/ dāre thĕ/ crŷstāl
Rāmpărt/(of) rāin ānd (the)/bōt/ / tŏmlĕss/ mōat ŏf/ thūndēr
Īf ŏn(ly)/nōw yōu/ wōuld/ / cŏme Ĭ/shōuld bĕ/hāppȳ
     Nōw ĭf nŏw/ ōnlȳ.

Here, though the movement is that of the natural speaking voice, and though there is a compelling sense of rhythm, even an uninstructed reader, one feels, would realize that any attempt to transcribe these slow, sad, dragging movements, these prolongations, into orthodox stress-syllable metrics would be pointless, as well as very difficult. A poem like this reminds us of the extraordinary flexibility of the English language and also makes us feel that quantitative metrics, handled as MacNeice handles them here, with a certain instinctive freedom, may have a wider future in English poetry than that of mere scholarly experiment.

These attempts at Horatian metres are, I think, the most interesting kinds of quantitative verse in English. Because it was used by Homer and Virgil, the hexameter has been popular. It is a line of six feet, dactyls or spondees at choice for the first four feet: normally a dactyl in the fifth foot, always a spondee in the sixth. It has been imitated not only with an attempt at keeping quantitative feet but with the substitution of stress-syllable feet for quantitative feet: spondees, in this accentual hexameter, tending to become trochees. It is not a particularly attractive line in English, in either its quantitative or stress-syllable versions, though the latter can be used for comic and satirical narrative, as by Clough, or for straightforward slightly sentimental story-telling as by Longfellow in *Evangeline* and *The Courtship of Miles Standish*. Here is an Elizabethan pair of quantitative hexameters, from Ascham's *Schoolmaster*:

Āll trāve/ lērs dō/ glādlў rĕ/pōrt grēat/prāise ŏf Ŭ/lȳssēs
Fōr thăt hĕ/ knēw mănў/ mēn's mān/nērs ānd/ sāw mănў/ cītīes.

This makes a decent attempt to accommodate quantities to ordinary English speech patterns, but of course the last syllables of 'trávellêrs' and 'mánnêrs' are only long by a fiction; the *r* is not consonantal, and the final plural *s* is in fact a z-sound. Both syllables are very short and probably were so in Elizabethan

English. The real quantities are 'trāvĕlĕrs' or 'trāv'lĕrs' and 'mānn/ĕrs'. Longfellow in his accentual hexameters gets something with much more of a run to it:

> Lóng wĭth/ín hăd bĕen/ spréad thĕ/ snów-whĭte/ clóth ŏn thĕ/ táblĕ;
> Theré stoŏd thĕ/ whéatĕn/loáf, ańd thĕ/ hónĕy/ frágrańt wĭth/ wíld
>   flòwers

He unhesitatingly substitutes stress-syllable trochees but it strengthens these lines that two of the 'strong' trochees 'snów-whìte' and 'wíld flòwers' are clearly also genuine English quantitative spondees, 'snōw-whīte' and 'wīld flōwers' ('flowers' is here clearly, though not of course in all its appearance in English verse, a word of one long syllable). Saintsbury is condescendingly kind about the *Evangeline* line, calling it 'a popular, tunable sort of rhythm' but thinks that like all long English dactylic stress-syllable lines it tends to be latently anapaestic. This can be seen in the last line of the passage he quotes if one takes the opening 'Ah!' as an anacrusis.

> Áh!/ ŏn hĕr spír/ĭt wĭthín/ ă déep/ĕr shád/ŏw hăd fáll(en).

It is the latent anapaestic run that gives the *Evangeline* line its combination, an attractive though slightly mechanical combination, of bounciness and smoothness. Clough, aiming more at stress-syllable spondees, has a heavier line, and if he does not achieve real stress-syllable spondees (whose very possibility is denied by the Trager-Smith school) has plenty of 'strong' stress-syllable trochees, which are genuinely quantitatively spondaic:

> Í wăs quîte/ ríght làst/ níght, ĭt/ ís tòo/ soón, tòo/ sùddĕn.

Though less mechanical than Longfellow's accentual hexameter, Clough's gains its greater flexibility and expressiveness at the cost of greater ambiguity. Taken in isolation this line could be easily scanned either,

Î wás/ quîte ríght/ làst níght, /ît ís/ tòo sóon,/ tòo súdd(en),

that is, as a straight run of iambic feet: or as a run of straight trochees, which, though more awkward, is not quite impossible:

Î wàs/ quíte rîght/ làst nîght,/ ít îs/ tóo soòn,/ tóo sùddèn.

One would have to make a case for the first or proper scansion on the grounds that it represents much more aptly than the iambic and trochaic ones the sense emphasis of the line.

Saintsbury thinks that there is in the natural genius of the English language an '*impatience* of classical form'. Broadly, in spite of the attractiveness of the MacNeice example here, one agrees with him. But attempts to imitate 'classical form' are likely to recur, and I hope this section shows that the scansion of such attempts is not such a difficult, or even impossible, task as young lovers of English poetry with no grounding in Greek or Latin prosody sometimes fear it to be.

PURE SYLLABIC METRE

There are languages, of which French is possibly one, but of which Japanese is a clearer and simpler example, in which stress differences and differences in the quantity of syllables are so slight, or so little observed, that they play no part in metrics. In such languages it is syllable count (with the addition in French verse of rhyme) which defines the lines of verse. Japanese is a language of short open syllables. Japanese poetry cannot use rhyme or alliteration to define a line of verse, not because rhyme or alliteration do not occur in Japanese, but because they occur so constantly in ordinary speech that they are not felt as aesthetically significant. The most famous type of Japanese poem consists of a line of five followed by a line of seven followed by another line of five syllables. It is called the haiku. These are seasonal poems. The first line depicts a scene; the second sets a moving actor, or action, against the scene; the third fuses scene and actor or action. The technique is purely presentational, or, as we might say in English, *imagist* (the early Imagist poets, Hulme, Flint, and Pound, owed a great deal to French prose versions of the Japanese haiku). The poet makes no overt comment, and indeed the Japanese, for all their love of nature, consider poets like Wordsworth, who comment a great deal, as using in poetry material more proper for meditative or philosophical prose.

Let us look now at the most famous of all Japanese haiku, Basho's poem on the Frog and the Pond. Syllabic scansion is very simple, one merely puts numbers over the syllables:

Furuike ya

(Furuike =(the) (an) old pond(s) Ya = Yes, and . . .)

Kawazu tobikomu

(Kawazu = (the) (a) frog(s) tobikomu = (roughly) jumping)

Mizo no oto.

(Mizo = (the) water no = our apostrophe *s* 's oto=noise)

1 2 3 4 5

Fu ru i ke ya

1 2 3 4 5 6 7

Ka wa zu to bi ko mu

1 2 3 4 5

Mi zo no o to.

The vowel sounds are more or less as in Italian, and are all short.

Though writing English haiku has lately become a very popular pastime, it is clear that the exact prosodic and aesthetic effect of a Japanese haiku can hardly be reproduced. Such a translation as this, for—instance,

1 2 3 4 5

The old pond, yes, and

1 2 3 4 5 6 7
A frog is jumping into
1 2 3 4 5
The water, and splash,

cannot help having stress patterns

The old pónd, yés, and
A frog is júmping ínto
The wáter, and splásh,

not present in Japanese. One might get a little nearer to the light movement of the original by lessening the *number* of syllables in each English line, but even then one would not be *very* near:

1 2 3 4
Old pond, yes, and
1 2 3 4 5
Frog jumping into
1 2 3 4
The water's noise.

1 2 3
Old pond, yes,
1 2 3 4
Frog there jumping,
1 2 3
Water's noise.

These two shorter versions get more of the effect of Japanese syntax, what I call the condensed vagueness, but they are still all, in English pure stress metrics, strong two-stress lines. Purely syllabic metrics seems, therefore, not suitable to the prosody of English as a natural language. Yet over a period of perhaps forty years a number of distinguished poets have been writing poems in what they think of as pure syllabics: Marianne Moore, the pioneer, and the most distinguished poet in this mode: Elizabeth Daryush, the daughter of Robert Bridges: W. H. Auden in some of the finest poems of his American period: Thom Gunn, who has studied under Yvor Winters at Stanford, and might be considered a mid-Atlantic poet; and, in Ireland and England, Richard Murphy, B. S. Johnson and George MacBeth. There is a definite vogue for syllabics, which we must look into.

An English-speaking poet who chooses to write in pure syllable-count metre is not, of course, attempting to abolish the phonetics and prosody of natural English speech. He is simply setting up a new pattern to *define* the English verse line. His intention, at first, may be hard to grasp. We have seen that it is usually possible to interpret a five-foot stress-syllable, or accentual foot line, especi-ally in actual performance, *as if* it were a four-stress pure sense-stress line. Pure sense stress metre is, in a way, the most *natural* metre in English. Similarly, stress-syllable metre, though artificial, is slightly more 'natural' in English than quantitative metre, and most exercises in quantitative metrics can be re-interpreted, especially in performance, as if they were in slightly unusual stress-syllable lines. We use pure sense stress all the time in speaking or reading English; we consciously discriminate accentual or stress-syllable feet only when reading and sometimes perhaps only when scanning verse; and we probably attend consciously to quantitative feet only when reading verse that we have been cued to read as English quantitative verse. Syllabic count units are not something we are ordinarily conscious of at all, and in fact it is characteristic of English though not of North American speech to slur or elide many syllables of low or insignificant stress in certain long words. There are also quite a number of diphthongal English words ending in *r* or *-er*, like 'flower', 'power', 'hour', 'tire', 'fire', which poets using stress-syllable metre can use either as disyllables or monosyllables at their convenience. The syllable, clearly, is a much more shifty and ambiguous element of speech in English than in Japanese.

These are strong theoretical arguments against the possibility of pure syllabic verse being very successful in the very varying patterns of educated English, in these islands. It has flourished most in the United States. In American speech, syllables tend even when weak to be unslurred, vowels and diphthongs to approximate in quantity and colour, and speech intonation, speech tunes, seem to an English ear to be much flatter, more level, more monotonous in a way, than English speech tunes. Syllables of main sense stress seem to get less emphasis than in standard educated English speech, syllables of secondary, tertiary and minimal stress rather more.

The poet Donald Davie, who has recently emigrated to California, has noted in an article in *The Listener* the lack of tone or tonality in American speech. We convey, or used to convey, in English English, much about our attitudes, our social position, our feelings towards those we are talking to by what we loosely call 'tone of voice'. We send signals out by the noises we make. The pattern of American speech, with its tendency to iron out regional and class differences, makes for what one could call a freedom and equality between syllabic units; and it is perhaps no accident that the pioneers of pure syllabic metrics in this century, like Marianne Moore, have been Americans. The one obvious aesthetic advantage of pure syllabic metrics over the more traditional kinds seems to me to be the impression it can convey of a very flat and dry, but also very painstaking, precision.

Many of Marianne Moore's earlier poems were in free verse. She seems, however, at an early stage to have felt the need for a more formal structuring (I owe these remarks to a brilliant pupil of mine, Betty Diamond, whose pioneer long study of Miss Moore's verse will I hope soon be published).

Here are two stanzas from a fairly early poem of Miss Moore's, in lines of (they are five-line stanzas) successively six, twelve, seven, ten, and fourteen syllables: I get the count exact by allowing the short vowel of 'the others' to elide or vanish. Notice, however, that 'ac-tu-al' has its full three syllables where even in moderately cultivated English-English speech it is often compressed into the ugly disyllable 'áck-shàll'.

```
         1  2   3   4    5    6
       'Taller by the length of
 1   2   3 4  5  6  7   8   9   10  11  12
a conversation of five hundred years than all
               1  2   3    4    5    6   7
             th(e) others, there was one whose tales
             1   2   3   4 5   6   7 8   9   10
             of what could never have been ac(-)tu(-)al
       1   2  3  4   5  6   7   8  9  10 11 12 13   14
     were better than the haggish uncompanionable drawl
     1  2 3 4   5  6
     of certitude; his by-
       1   2   3   4 5 6 7  8 9 10 11 12
     play was more terrible in its effectiveness
            1   2   3   4    5  6  7
          than the fiercest front attack.
            1   2   3   4   5   6    7  8  9  10
          The staff, the bag, the feigned inconsequence
     1   2  3   4   5  6  7   8    9   10  11 12 13 14
     of manner, best bespeak that weapon, self-protectiveness.
```

One should notice that a number of these lines can be scanned as quite regular stress-syllable lines. Thus,

Thán thě/ fiércěst/ frónt ått/áck

could be a trochaic tetrameter, of the stress-syllable kind, with the last foot truncated. If we do not make Miss Moore's elision,

Thě óth/ ěr, thére/ wǎs oné/ whǒse táles

is a perfectly regular iambic tetrameter. A line like

Ǒf whát/ coǔld név/ ěr háve/ beěn áct/ ǔál

or

Thě stáff/ thě bág/ thě feígned/ iňcóns/ěquénce

has in either case a perfectly regular iambic beat. If we respect Miss Moore's intentions, we do not give the lines this heavy and isolating beat and instead take the whole movement (syntactical, semantic, as well as syllabically counted) of the stanza as the metrical unit; but here, as often before, we can notice how in approaching a new and experimental type of metrics we (and the poet also, perhaps) lean a little on a more familiar type.

Marianne Moore is a poet who uses pure syllabics, in an apt phrase of Miss Diamond's, to 'avoid direct frontal attack'. W. H. Auden is a poet who is rarely concerned with this sort of avoidance, a very direct and frontal poet in his attack on the reader, indeed. He has made brilliant uses of pure syllabic verse for quite different purposes. Alonso's speech to Ferdinand in Auden's variation or commentary on Shakespeare's *The Tempest*, *The Sea and the Mirror*, is in a stanza of eleven nine-syllable lines and a twelfth seven-syllable line, rhyming aabbcddefefc: because stresses are not counted in pure syllabics the rhymes can be on syllables of minor stress, can be what are called in stress-syllable verse off-stress rhymes. Since there is not what may be called a 'natural' nine-syllable line in English stress-syllable metre (other than an iambic tetrameter with a feminine ending, or an iambic penta-meter starting with a truncated foot, such as is sometimes found in Chaucer) there is comparatively little danger of Auden's nine-syllable lines being taken as regular iambics:

> 1   2   3   4   5   6 7 8   9
> Dear Son, when the warm multitudes cry
> 1 2   3   4   5 6 7 8 9
> Ascend your throne majestical*ly*,
> 1   2   3   4   5 6 7 8   9
> But keep in mind the waters where fish
> 1   2   3 4 5 6   7   8   9
> See sceptres descending with no wish

```
  1     2     3     4  5  6 7  8 9
To touch them; sit regal and erect,
  1  2  3  4  5   6       7  8  9
But imagine the sands where a crown
   1  2   3 4 5 6  7 8   9
Has the status of a broken-down
  1 2 3   4 5 6 7   8   9
Sofa or mutilated stat*ue*:
  1    2   3  4  5     6   7  8  9
Remember as bells and cannon boom
   1   2    3    4    5  6 7 8  9
The cold deep that does not envy you
   1    2    3   4 5 6 7  8    9
The sunburnt superficial kingdom
    1     2  3  4  5  6  7
Where a king is an ob*ject*.
```

I have italicized there the off-stress rhymes; in performance I
would also make the 'you' of 'envy you' an off-stress rhyme,
saying 'énvў yŏu' rather than 'énvў yóu': but I think this choice
of a stress pattern is imposed by my sense of rhetorical tact, not
by Auden's metrics. When we look more closely at this nine-
syllable line we notice that it tends to divide into phrasal members
of three syllables:

> See sceptres/ descending/ with no wish . . .
> Remember/ as bells and/ cannon boom . . .
> The cold deep/ that does not/ envy you . . .

but that these phrasal members resist interpretation as stress-
syllable feet. If we have a sense of what might be called 'underlying' stress-syllable feet, these are two-syllable ones, iambic or
trochaic:

> Ăscénd/ yoŭr thróne/ măjést/ĭcál (ly)

or

> Hás thĕ/státŭs/ óf ă/ brókĕn-/dówn . . .

For Auden here, as for Marianne Moore, pure syllabics gives a combination of flexibility with formality; but in his case we are much more aware of the formal element than in hers, and more aware of a 'latent' or 'underlying' stress-syllable rhythm.

Experiments in ten-syllable lines tend to be less successful than Auden's nine-syllable line because we are much tempted to scan the ten-syllable line as traditional iambics, or, failing that, to try to interpret it as a pure stress line. There was a long correspondence in *The Times Literary Supplement* in the mid-1950s about a poem in Richard Murphy's *Sailing to an Island*, the poem 'The Woman of the House'. Murphy intended this to be in pure decasyllabic quatrains.

> 1   2   3 4 5   6   7   8 9   10
> On a patrician evening in Ireland
> 1   2   3   4   5   6   7   8   9 10 11 12
> I was born in the guest-room; she delivered me.
>   1   2 3 4 5 6   7   8   9   10
> May I deliver her from the cold hand
>   1   2   3   4   5   6 7 8   9   10
> Where now she lies, with a brief elegy?

Ignoring the fact that the second line has twelve syllables, a difficulty here is that the lines can be scanned quite plausibly as freely handled iambic pentameters:

> Ón å/ påtríc/iån év/ éníng/ iň Íre(land)
> Í wås/ bórn în/ thě gúest-/roòm; she/ dělív/ erěd mé.
> Måy Í/ dělív/ěr hér/ frôm thě/ còld hánd
> Whère nów/ shě líes/ wìth å/ brìef él/ěgý?

There is no substitution there, not even the trochee in the sensitive second foot of the second line, for which we have not seen precedents. The suggested scansion would not lead to a wrong performance, but once we got into the poem we might begin, after two or three stanzas, to feel that the stress-syllable iambic pentameter is not what is intended. In writing in to *The Times Literary*

Supplement to defend Richard Murphy, who had been accused of failing to master traditional metrics, I made, however, the opposite mistake of supposing that his intention was to write four-stress lines in pure stress metre on, roughly, the Langland model but using occasional rhyme instead of alliteration. My scansion would have been:

> Ón a patrícian: évening in Íreland
> I was bórn in the gúest-room: shé delívered me.
> May I delíver hér: from the cóld hánd
> Where nów she líes : with a bríef élegy.

I still think that scansion is nearer than the slightly tricky iambic one to how one should perform these lines. Murphy intended neither scansion, and intended one *not* to expect regular iambic lines, but could not have expected one to exclude speech-stress. B. S. Johnson, on the other hand, another young poet who has experimented with pure syllabic decasyllables tells me that he knows many of his decasyllables turn into fairly regular iambic pentameters – an iambic run is common enough, after all, in ordinary English speech rhythms. It may be that in the long run the main use of recent experiments in pure syllabic metres will not be to replace either stress-syllable metres, pure stress metres, or experiments in English quantitative metres, but to give our handling of these a greater flexibility.

It is prudent for the experimenter to avoid syllable counts that are too much associated with regular iambic stress-syllable scansion. The odd numbers, like seven and nine, are more amenable to syllabics than the evens like eight and ten. Thom Gunn, in his syllabic experiments in *My Sad Captains*, gets good results with seven-syllable quatrains with off-stress rhymes which are often also half-rhymes:

> 1 2 3 4 5 6 7
> I am approaching. Past dry

```
1       2  3   4   5   6    7
towers softly seeding from mere
 1 2 3 4  5   6  7
delicacy of age, I
 1   2    3    4     5   6   7
penetrate, through thickets, or
 1 2   3    4    5    6    7
over warm herbs my feet press
 1   2     3   4 5   6     7
to brief potency. Now with
 1    2     3    4  5   6 7
the green quickness of grasses
 1   2   3    4    5   6   7
mingles the smell of the earth. . . .
```

Here is a natural movement, seeming to suit the theme of the tentative exploration of nature, and the lines firmly resist scanning as either trochaic tetrameters with the last foot truncated or iambic trimeters with feminine endings.

We have studied now all the possible modes of constructing a line of verse in English, by pure stress metre, by stress-syllable or accentual foot metre, by quantitative metre (or by accentual imitations of quantitative foot patterns), and by pure syllabic count. We have seen that pure stress metre is more natural than any other metre to English, but that it does not permit such delicacies of modulation as stress-syllable metre; we have seen that quantitative metre is not very natural to English, but can be written fairly successfully, though it generally lends itself to misinterpretation, by an unlearned ear, as stress-syllable metre of a slightly unusual kind. Finally, we have seen that the nature of the English language – including the ambiguity of our working definition of a syllable – makes pure syllabic metre in theory very unsuitable to English, and yet that some distinguished recent poets have used it very effectively. I have tried, without using the technical terms of scientific phonetics, to emphasize the close relationship of metrical patterns to the patterns, particularly the sense-stress patterns, of English speech. The best use that a young reader could make of this book so far is not in using my methods to scan verse that I have not quoted but in trying to construct verses of his own on the various principles I have described. We are near the end of our journey. Rhyme, compared to rhythm, is a simple topic; and free verse, to which I will devote a brief final chapter, will always be found, when it works, to be not really 'free' but to be an adaptation of one of the four metrical principles I have described – stress verse, stress-syllable verse, quantitative verse, pure syllabic verse. No other principles of versification than these are available, as far as I can make out, in the English language.

I have left out of consideration in this little book what is some-times called liturgical prose: the psalms, for instance, and other poetic passages, as they occur in the Anglican Prayer Book or the Authorized Version of the Bible. The strongly poetical effect of these depends on rhetorical parallelism – 'Tell it not in Gath, publish it not in the streets of Askalon' – rather than on any purely metrical principle. Liturgical prose can be used as a vehicle for writing of a highly poetic sort: as in David Jones's *The Anathemata* or in T. S. Eliot's translation of Perse's *Anabasis*. Claudel wrote much of his work in long sentences of liturgical prose, which in French are called *versets*, and which we might call versicles. But, however aesthetically interesting liturgical prose is, it is not *verse*, in the perhaps rather narrow but I think practically useful sense of this treatise.

5
Rhyme

In pure stress verse we saw that the function of alliteration was to link two half lines of verse together and to define, or isolate, the two linked halves as a line of verse, not a piece of prose. In Skelton, the two half lines became separate two stress lines and were linked by end-rhymes, sometimes a great string of these, instead of by alliteration. Broadly speaking the main function of rhyme in English stress-syllable verse is the same as the function of alliteration: to define or isolate the individual line of verse, and also to link different lines of verse together. But the linkages possible through rhyme are of a much more various and interesting kind than the linkages possible through alliteration. I think it impossible, unless the English language undergoes very great changes, that any English poet should in the foreseeable future write a line of verse which is not basically either a pure stress line, a stress-syllable line, a quantitative line (or an accentual imitation of one) or a line based metrically on syllable count. But any poet at any time may invent a new stanza form, or may alter the various traditional arrangements of rhyme in a form like the sonnet. And if we make allowance, as we did in the last chapter, for off-stress rhyme and half-rhyme or off-rhyme, for assonance and consonance, our notion of what rhyme is and can do will be enlarged: we can also profit by extending our idea of the position of rhyme. It is only by a convention, for instance, that lines of verse rhyme at the end rather than at the beginning; and internal rhyme is a common and effective phenomenon.

In traditional English stress-syllable verse, however, rhyme is usually at the end of the line, and two words are said to rhyme when their main vowel, of main stress, and any consonants which may follow it, coincide, but their initial consonant or consonants are different: as *no, so, can, ban, long, song, length, strength*. Words which are exactly the same in sound though different in sense, like *rose*, the flower, and *rose*, the preterite of the verb *rise*, are not thought proper rhymes in English, though in French verse, as *rime riche*, they are an ornament: we accept, however, rhymes like *rose* and *grows*, *love* and *glove*. Such rhymes on one strong syllable are called masculine rhymes. Rhymes like *pretty* and *witty*, *roses* and *poses*, are called feminine rhymes: rhymes like *niminy*, *piminy, prettily, wittily, rosily, cosily*, are called triple rhymes, and their use is generally confined to light or comic verse. Rhymes of more than three syllables, like *visibility, risibility*, can be found or invented but their use is confined to very broadly comic, sometimes music-hall or patter verse.

English is less rich in rhymes than many other languages. *Amore* in Italian rhymes with *cuore*, but *love* in English perfectly only with the undignified word *shove* or the trivial word *glove* (itself a disguised *rime riche*). The word *God*, as full of richness as *love* in meaning, has its aptest rhymes in *odd* ('How odd/ Of God/ To choose/The Jews') and *sod* (under which one is buried, hoping to meet one's God, or rest in His bosom). *Death* monotonously suggests *breath*, *moon* equally monotonously *June*. *Stream, gleam, dream* are another set that cling too obviously together. This is one reason why a number of courtesy rhymes, rhymes to the eye rather than the ear, like *love, move* have been traditionally accepted in English versification, and why a number of modern poets, from Wilfred Owen onwards, have sought out some substitute for the traditional concept of rhyme. It should also be added that English, a language 'clogged with consonants', full of words ending in very stiff consonantal clusters – think of the word, for which fortunately there is no rhyme, *sixths* – is much less suited for writing simple tuneful songs in than

languages like Italian or the Lowland Scots vernacular of Burns
that are full of words with open vocalic endings. Compare:

> O never look down, my lassie, at a',
> O, never look down, my lassie, at a',
> Thy lips are as sweet, and thy figure complete,
> As the finest dame in castle or ha',

by Burns, with the complete loss of lilt which we get when we
simply add the English consonants, and truncate the diminutive
'lassie':

> O never look down, my lass, at all,
> O, never look down, my lass, at all,
> Thy lips are as sweet, and thy figure complete,
> As the finest dame in castle or hall.

Every charm is gone; in particular the truncation of 'lassie'
destroys the suggestion, rather than fact, of quadruple rhyme:
'*Lass*ie, at *a*', 'and '*Cast*le or *ha*'. Where English, on the other
hand, excels is not in this musical use of rhyme but in the sharp,
pointed use of rhyme (and here the clustered consonantal endings
can help) to point sense: this is particularly so in the heroic
couplet, and here are some good examples of the rhyme of wit
and surprise from Pope:

> But ne'er one sprig of laurel graced these ribalds
> From slashing Bentley down to piddling Tibbalds . . .
>
> Rufa, whose eye quick-glancing o'er the Park
> Attracts each light gay meteor of a Spark,
> Agrees as ill with Rufa studying Locke,
> As Sappho's diamonds with her dirty smock. . . .
>
> Now deep in Taylor and the Book of Martyrs,
> Now drinking citron with his Grace and Chartres,
> Now conscience chills her, and now passion burns:
> And Atheism and Religion take their turns.

The contrast of the Pope and the Burns passages reinforces a point I made earlier: though of course there are great English songs and song-writers, still on the whole the greatest English poetry tends to be dramatic, narrative, reflective, or descriptive and to be written for the speaking rather than the singing voice. (And this is true of many poems which we might conventionally call 'lyrical': Shakespeare's sonnets and Keats's odes, for instance, are for the speaking voice.)

Geoffrey N. Leech in *A Linguistic Guide to English Poetry*, has tabulated possible kinds of rhyme thus. His formula for a rhyme is Consonant-Vowel-Consonant, but he points out that there may be from none up to three consonants before the vowel (*strength* is an example of three consonants before the vowel), and from none up to four consonants after it (*sixths*, which is pronounced *siksths*, is an example of four consonants after it). We then get six types of sound parallelism within pairs of syllables. The unvarying parts are here italicized.

(1) Alliteration: *Consonant*-Vowel-Consonant. *G*reat, *g*row.

(2) Assonance. Consonant-*Vowel*-Consonant. Gr*ea*t, f*ai*l.

(3) Consonance. Consonant-Vowel-*Consonant*. Grea*t*, mea*t*.

(4) Reverse rhyme. *Consonant-Vowel*-Consonant. *Gra*t, *gra*ze.

(5) Pararhyme. *Consonant*-Vowel-*Consonant*. *Gr*eat, *gr*oat.

(6) Rhyme proper. Consonant-*Vowel-Consonant*. Gr*eat*, b*ait*.

A few remarks should be made about each of Leech's types. His formula for alliteration covers the very simple Anglo-Saxon type but not the Welsh type, much more complex, of which there are sometimes echoes in English poetry, for instance in Wordsworth's line

The *sl*eepless *s*ou*l*/ that *p*erished in his *pr*ide

where the formula in the first half of the line is two consonants followed by a vowel, then the first consonant followed by a vowel followed by the second consonant: and the second half of the line, '*per*ished', '*pr*ide' is a mirror-image reversal of the same formula. Wordsworth probably hit on this formula by a happy accident but Hopkins had studied Welsh poetry and gives us something more showy, if not intrinsically more successful, in the line

And *fr*ightful a nightfall *f*olded *r*ueful a day,

where the two initial alliterating consonants of 'frightful' are split up between two subsequent strongly stressed syllables. Both these examples, though unusual in English, would, my Welsh friends tell me, be considered rather crude and inept in Welsh. The American critic Kenneth Burke has attempted to widen our idea of alliteration by pointing out that there is a certain affinity, as we discover when we have a bad cold in the nose, between *m* and *b* and between *n* and *d* both in initial and forward positions. We can try the theory out, somewhat blasphemously, with two famous lines of Shakespeare's:

Whed to the sessiods of sweet siled thought
I call to mid rebebradce of things past.

Comic though Burke's idea seems it is probably true that our sense of consonantal patterning and affinity in poetry extends much further than a perception of simple alliteration.

Of Leech's other types, assonance is frequent in ballad and folk poetry but comparatively rare in literate art poetry. It is sometimes found in a poet who had a strong folkish or balladic element, Hardy. Consonance includes what we have called courtesy rhyme, *love, move*, and also something very common in recent poetry deliberate off-rhyme or half-rhyme as when Yeats at the beginning of 'Easter, 1916' matches 'houses' with 'faces'. Consonance has appealed to modern poets because it much enlarges the possible range of English rhymes. There is no rhyme proper to 'orange', for instance, but it has off-stress consonance with 'syringe' and 'arrange'. There is no rhyme to the modern pronunciation of 'oblige' but it has on-stress consonance with such words as 'assuage' and 'rage'. It is sometimes difficult in a poet like Yeats, however, when he rhymes words like 'sun' and 'on' or 'that' and 'but' to know whether this is deliberate consonance or an imperfect rhyme, less imperfect to an Anglo-Irish than a native English ear. To my own Scottish ear Yeats's rhyme, with its burred final *r*,

> What voice more sweet than hers
> When young and beautiful
> She rode to harriers?

is very beautiful but most Southern English speakers I have consulted dislike it. We should remember that the great poets of this century have spoken many different variants of English, American, and Irish English. In Robert Frost, for instance, the past participle 'been', in a rhyming position, is always 'bin', as in Elizabethan English. In poetry of the past it is often wise to assume that what looks like imperfect rhyme or consonance, may have been a good rhyme in the pronunciation of the poet's time and place:

> Let the death-divining swan
> That defunctive music can . . .

> Here thou, Great Anna, whom three Realms obey,
> Dost sometimes Counsel take, and sometimes Tea.

> . . . by flatterers besieged,
> And so obliging that he ne'er obliged.

What Leech calls reverse rhyme is not something of which English poets make much conscious use, and he has had to invent a name for it. He means the kind of echo present in this line from Hopkins,

> *Que*lled or *que*nched, in *lea*ves the *lea*ping sun,

and he could perhaps have subsumed it under alliteration, as alliteration with vocalic echo. The phrase 'reverse rhyme' could have another more obvious sense. We can imagine a poem in couplets in which the poet rhymed *mate* with *tame*, *bark* with *crab*, *bad* with *dab*, and so on, and no doubt after a few couplets we would notice what he was up to; I do not think this has ever been consciously done in English verse, nor can I guess whether it would be much worth doing. It might be more interesting in the interior of a line, and including also reverse consonance, as an aid to phrase-making: *sagging gas*, *dearth of thread*, *load of dole*, *scudding dusk*, *black club*, are a few phrases involving reverse rhyme or consonance which spontaneously occur to me.

Pararhyme is like *rime riche* with the consonants the same, but the interior vowel changed. Its most famous English practitioner is Wilfred Owen, and Leech quotes some lines from 'Strange Meeting':

> It seemed that out of battle I e*scaped*
> Down some profound dull tunnel, long since *scooped*
> Through granites which titanic wars had *groined*.
> Yet also there encumbered sleepers *groaned* . . .

Though Owen discovered it on his own, it was often used, Leech tells us, in medieval Icelandic verse, and Owen's lines seem to me there to be in pure stress metre:

> It seémed that oút: of báttle I escáped
> Down some profóund dull túnnel: lóng since scóoped
> Through gránites which titánic: wárs had gróined
> Yet alsó there encúmbered: sléepers gróaned . . .

It suits the heavy, stark, unmodulated and repetitive movement of pure stress verse but would be out of place (because of the monotonously heavy sense emphasis on the last stressed syllable of the line) in stress-syllable verse, in which, so far as I know, it has never been successfully used. (At the same time, I must admit that some readers consider 'Strange Meeting' itself to be written in stress-syllable verse.)

It has been the aim of this book, as I have said already, to be suggestive rather than exhaustive, and to provide a rationale rather than a dictionary. Most books on metre have a chapter trying to take in at least a good range of English stanza forms, but it is my feeling that, whereas the scanning of a line of verse is always a tricky and difficult business in English, any fool, using the abab formula, can, confronted with a Shakespearian or a Petrarchan sonnet, quatrains, ottava rima stanzas, Spenserian stanzas, villanelles, terza rima, and so on, count rhyme endings, including repeated refrain endings, and make up his own mind about the aesthetic effects of the almost indefinitely various possibilities of English stanzaic formation. But a few very general and very dogmatic remarks may be of use. I think most of the stanzas and individual verse forms (like the sonnet) are made out of combinations of the two rhymed forms that seem most natural in English – the quatrain (abab) and the couplet (aa). Forms based on three-line units, like Italian terza rima or simplified variations of it, seem more difficult to handle in English. Shakespeare's sonnets, which are probably the greatest sonnets in the English language, consist in fact of three quatrains, abab, cdcd, efef, followed by a clinching couplet, gg. I find myself, and I think this is a common experience of lovers of poetry, that I have many of the first quatrains of Shakespeare's sonnets by heart, but not the second or the third quatrains, and that, re-reading the sonnets, I often find the clinching couplet trite and disappointing. The proper Italian sonnet rhymes abbaabba, with only two rhymes in the octave (or eight-line first part) and with a variation of two or three other rhymes in the sestet (six-line part), arranged variously, but never so that the last two lines rhyme unless they rhyme with the first line of the sestet. There should be a break in sense between the octave and the sestet, though Milton, one of our greatest sonnet writers, did not always observe this. But Milton's and Wordsworth's sonnets have more formal complex unity than Shakespeare's and if one has any part of them by heart, one probably has them by heart as wholes. The octave tends to have an asserting and advancing, the sestet a receding and conceding movement, rather like wave motions on the shore. Hopkins is the fourth notable English sonnet writer whom one would mention, but one feels that his sonnets are often great poems rather than great sonnets.

If we take the quatrain and the couplet as the two primary English stanza forms, the aesthetic quality of the couplet is clinchingness, a tightness, rightness, and condensation,

> Thy hand, great Anarch, lets the curtain fall:
> And universal darkness buries all.

The quality of the quatrain, as Dr Johnson noted, though not precisely in these words, is a certain spaciousness and grandeur:

> Full many a gem of purest ray serene
> The dark unfathomed caves of ocean bear:
> Full many a flower is born to blush unseen
> And waste its sweetness on the desert air.

Most longer stanzas, as I have said, are combinations of these, or are sometimes, like the stanzas of most of Keats's odes, cut down from the sonnet (the first quatrain of the sonnet, plus the sestet: in *Ode to a Nightingale*, the second last line is shortened; in *To Autumn* an extra line is added to the sestet, giving a couplet before the last line and an eleven-line stanza). Three-line units or terzets or tercets are less easy to handle in English, partly because of the continuity of rhyme they demand: true terza rima, as in Dante, is aba bcb cdc ded, and so on indefinitely. The only really distinguished uses of this metre I know are by Wyatt, who introduces it in his free versions of Alemanni's satires in the mid-sixteenth century and by Shelley in his great unfinished poem *The Triumph of Time*. Binyon used it competently in his version of Dante, but with considerable use of inversion and also of feminine rhyme. Eliot imitated its effect, but did not follow its form, in a notable passage in *Little Gidding* modelled on one in Dante. A succession of terza rima terzets, four of them, followed not by a fifth terzet but by a couplet, can also be used to create an irregular sonnet form, more rapid and flexible than the usual sonnet form, as in the stanzas of Shelley's *Ode to the West Wind*:

O Wild West Wind, thou breath of Autumn's being,	*a*
Thou, from whose unseen presence the leaves dead	*b*
Are driven, like ghosts from an enchanter fleeing,	*a*
Yellow, and black, and pale, and hectic red,	*b*
Pestilence-stricken multitudes: O thou,	*c*
Who chariotest to their dark wintry bed	*b*
The winged seeds, where they lie cold and low,	*c*
Each like a corpse within its grave, until	*d*
Thine azure sister of the Spring shall blow	*c*
Her clarion o'er the dreaming earth, and fill	*d*
(Driving sweet buds like flocks to feed in air)	*e*
With living hues and odours plain and hill:	*d*
Wild Spirit, which art moving everywhere;	*e*
Destroyer and preserver; hear, oh, hear!	*e*

It suggests the difficulty of this form in English that even in his first stanza, Shelley has two imperfect rhymes: 'thou' with 'low' and 'blow' and 'air' and 'everywhere' with 'hear'. It should be noticed also that this terza rima fourteen-line stanza has a continuous rapidity that neither the Shakespearian nor the Petrarchan sonnet possess; it arouses expectation, it seems to lead on to the next stanza, whereas, even in a sonnet sequence that tells a more or less clear story, like Sidney's *Astrophel to Stella*, each sonnet tends to seem a more or less self-contained unit, a discrete short poem, in itself.

Even more than in the case of discriminating between different kinds of metre in English, it will help the young reader to attempt to build up various stanza forms for himself, exploring their possibilities, much more than to go through anthologies marking the margins with *a*s, *b*s and *c*s. Nothing can be more boring than simply attempting to learn the rhyme schemes of various kinds of regular rhymed poem by heart; but, looking into the more elaborate stanza forms, or short poem forms like the sonnet and the villanelle, it may be useful to distinguish the bricks, couplets, quatrains, tercets, out of which the more elaborate forms are built.

6
Free Verse

The term free verse can be used in very wide ways. The late Herbert Read thought that in their blank verse at its best Wordsworth and Keats were writing what is practically free verse; he was not making allowances for the great flexibility, the readiness to accept substitution, of the English five-foot iambic line. A poem like Milton's *Lycidas* or Wordsworth's *Ode on Intimations of Immortality*, which has no fixed stanza length or rhyme scheme, which allows for 'hanging' or unrhymed lines, and the interspersion irregularly of shorter lines among longer ones, is in a sense 'free'. Some critics would use the term for any poem they admire which does not seem to be written in regular iambics. Yeats, for instance, was a very great, though as we have seen in one sense a very 'free' and flexible, master of traditional iambic metrics. But I came recently on an attempt to scan the opening line of one of his greater late poems, *Byzantium*, thus:

The únpúrged ímages of dáy recéde.

Yeats was praised by the writer for cramming the first three metrical stresses of the iambic pentameter together, and spacing out the last two. If he had done so, he would have indeed been writing a kind of free verse. But if we use our simplified version of the Trager-Smith four-stress system, we see that the line scans perfectly regularly thus:

1 2 3 4 1 2 1 4 1 4
The un/purged im/ages of day/ recede,

or, in my other equivalent notation, thus:

Thĕ ûn/pùrged ím/ăgês/ ŏf dáy/ rĕcéde.

Even if we want to give a stronger sense stress to 'un-' than I think rhetorically justified, such a scansion as

$$\begin{matrix} 1 & 3 & 3 & 4 \end{matrix}$$
The un/purged im/ . . .

is still regular and permissible. I think the critic to whom I am alluding was mislead by the possible four-stress pure-stress scansion which can always be felt as underlying the iambic line:

The únpurged ímages: of dáy recéde.

Much that is taken as free verse, or as breaking the old rules, is merely, in fact, an intelligent use of the great flexibility of the old rules. But there are, of course, important poets who unlike Yeats set out to write what they would call *vers libre* or free verse, and it is with them that we must be concerned.

Poets of the mid- or late-nineteenth century, like Whitman and Henley, had experimented with unrhymed poems in lines of irregular length, and even a poet like Matthew Arnold, very conscious of regular form, had written some pleasant poems in short unrhymed lines of no fixed length or metrical pattern. The free verse of this century derives, however, less from these than from the Imagist movement. This had its roots in a group of obscure but interesting poets, some – Tancred, Campbell, Stoner – now completely forgotten; two others, T. E. Hulme and F. S. Flint, remembered more as theorists and innovators than as poets in their own right, who used to meet at an institution called the Poets' Club around 1907 and 1908. They were bored by late Victorian verse, in particular by the rhetorical padding, the otiose adjectives, imposed by adhering to a regular iambic line and a regular rhyme scheme. They were interested in the Japanese haiku, in the epigrams of Herrick, in the parallelism of Biblical poetry; and both Flint and Hulme knew something about the theories and practice of Gustave Kahn, a minor poet but a copious propagandist, in France, for the theory of *vers libre*. The young American poet Ezra Pound met this group when he came to England from Venice in 1908, but he was then writing a very different type of poetry, based on his study of Swinburne, Rossetti, William Morris, and some of the English poets of the 1890s, and on his work as a university student in the United States on medieval and Renaissance poetry in the Romance languages. It was not till around 1912 that he caught up with the forgotten movement of 1908, invented and publicized the term Imagism and gathered under his banner a few younger poets like Richard Aldington and H. D. Pound, always restless, soon dissociated himself from Imagism as a movement, calling himself instead a Vorticist. In England Imagism had a very short life, though two English poets, Herbert Read and Basil Bunting, can be considered as disciples of Pound. In the United States, in the shorter poems of William Carlos Williams and later in those of poets of the Black Mountain School like Robert Creeley, Imagism, and particularly its 'free verse' element, had a much longer life and might be said to be still thriving. Pound's slightly younger friend Eliot had written his own earlier poems quite in ignorance of Imagism as a movement, but much influenced by the poems, sometimes in rhymed *vers libre*, of the French poet Jules Laforgue: later poems were to be influenced by the very free and flexible blank verse of Jacobean drama. Free verse in this century can thus be seen as a revolt against the deadness of decadent late Victorian and Edwardian versification and as a search for new models and ideas in many places. To concentrate, to cut out the dead wood, to present something (an 'image', or an immediate complex of feelings, rather than a logical process of thought or a complicated rhetorical exposition) as *economically* as possible was a common principle of all Imagists, and a practice of a number of free verse poets who would not have called themselves Imagists. But some free verse

F

poets, like D. H. Lawrence, used an opposite technique, based on the Bible and Whitman, of expansive repetition with variation, of rhetorical parallelism, rather than condensation: Herbert Read, as I have mentioned, did not think that Lawrence's free verse, any more than Whitman's, was really *verse*. He would have classified it as versicles, or as liturgical prose.

What I recognize as good free verse is verse which does not scan regularly but seems always on the verge of scanning regularly; which is neither strictly in pure stress metre, nor stress syllable metre, nor quantitative metre, nor pure syllabics, but which often seems to be getting near to one or other of these, perhaps attempting to fuse two of them, perhaps deliberately and abruptly alternating between one and another. One should add that poets in free verse tend to make a much more conscious use than more traditional poets of the pause, in the middle of lines, between blocks of lines, at the ends of lines: and that these pauses are indicated by a striking use of blank spaces and of long indentations on the printed page, a use which is sometimes described as 'visual scansion'.

There is a recent type of poem, the concrete poem, which is not intended to be read aloud at all, but to make a pleasing printed pattern on the page, a pattern often with semantic overtones. A simple example of the concrete poem is the following, adapted (one needs types of different colours and sizes) from one of Ian Hamilton Finlay's.

SAIL
S A I L
S A I L
S A I L O R

In its proper lay-out (or one of its proper lay-outs, for Finlay has published several variations of this) this makes a triangular pattern, rather like that of a triangular sail; and one may have a visual illusion of perspective, a little boat with a triangular sail is coming nearer and nearer to land, till at last one sees not only the sail but the sailor standing beside it. But, however ingenious and pleasing, concrete poems, it seems to me, fall outside the definition of versification as considered in this treatise.

I shall try now, in one deservedly famous passage of modern free verse to indicate not a scansion in the conventional sense but a kind of perpetual approach towards traditional regularity. The first poem that made the world aware of something new coming into English metrics was, probably, T. S. Eliot's *The Love Song of J. Alfred Prufrock*. The first lines set the note. I shall first make a simple pure stress scansion, using a mark for duple stress, which is as much in evidence here, I think, as in Kipling's *The Road to Mandalay*, which helps to give both poems their 'swing':

> Lét us gő then, yóu and Í
> Where the évening is spréad őut against the ský
> Like a pátient étherised upón a tăble;
> Let us gő, through cértain half-desérted stréets,
> The múttering retréats
> Or réstless niğhts in one-nìght chéap hotèls
> And săwdust réstaurants with őyster-shélls . . .

This would give some indication, as pure-stress scansion should, of the sense emphasis with which the lines should be read aloud: and we find a kind of regularity, at least two duple stresses to each line, two single stresses to each line except one very short one, and in one line the feeling that we should mark in two secondary stresses. But we also feel that traditional stress-syllable metre is being alluded to, even if it is finally being evaded, and we might try out such a scansion as this:

> Lét ŭs/ gó thĕn,/ yóu aňd/ Í
> Whére thĕ/éveniňg/ ĭs spréad óut/ ăgaínst/thĕ ský
> Líke ă/ pátiĕnt/éthĕr/isĕd ŭpón /ă táb(le);

Lĕt ŭs gó/ throŭgh cért/aĭn hálf/ dĕsért/ĕd stréets,
Thĕ mútt/ĕriñg/ rĕtreáts
Of rést/lĕss níghts/iñ óne-/ nĭght chéap/ hôtéls
Aṅd sáw/dŭst rést/aŭránts/ wĭth óys/tĕr-shélls. . . .

We get a trochaic tetrameter with the last foot truncated: an iambic pentameter with the first two feet, including the sensitive second foot, reversed, and trisyllabic substitution in the third foot: an iambic pentameter with the first *three* reversed, the fourth foot trisyllabic, and only the fifth foot regular (with a feminine, or extra-metrical, last syllable): then an iambic pentameter *perfectly* regular except for the trisyllabic substitution, traditionally quite permissible, in the first foot: then a regular iambic trimeter: and then two completely regular iambic pentameters. It seems to me that it is the last two lines that give us the sense of a basically regular iambic pattern which is being freely 'counterpointed' in Hopkins's sense but which the poet is always coming back to. And yet this stress-syllable scansion needs the pure stress scansion to supplement it: if we take the two scansions together they explain the sense of impudent bounce in these lines, the effect which critics have sometimes described as 'syncopation'.

This example may suggest, what I believe to be true, that 'free verse', where it is effective, depends in the poet on a mastery of traditional metrics that has more or less become second nature.

Eliot made this very remark about Ezra Pound and in a beautiful passage at the end of *Hugh Selwyn Mauberley* one comes on similar ambiguities of scansion, that seem nevertheless to be tied to a firm grasp of traditional metrics. Should one scan, in a Hopkins fashion, allowing for feet of four syllables to one syllable? Is it

Oř thróugh / daẘn- / míst
Thĕ gréy / aṅd róse
Of thĕ/ jŭríd/ ĭcál
Flám/ iṅgóes,

with alternating lines of three and two feet? Or is it

Oŕ thróúgh / dåwn-míst
Thĕ ́gréy/ and róse
Of the jůríd/ îcal
Flám/ îngóes,

with two main beats to a line? The uncertainty begets the delicacy.
But contrast with both Eliot and Pound the free verse of D. H.
Lawrence, in *Tortoise Shout*:

> I remember, when I was a boy,
> I heard the scream of a frog, which was caught
>   with his foot in the mouth of an
>   up-starting snake;
> I remember when I first heard bull-frogs break
>   into sound in the spring;
> I remember hearing a wild goose out of the
>   throat of the night
> Cry loudly, beyond the lake of waters. . . .

This can be spoken aloud very effectively, but the technique of
repetition and parallelism is rhetorical rather than metrical. One
could scan these fine lines, but there would be little point in doing
so.

Lawrence's rhetoric works, in a powerful accumulative way, but
not, as the Eliot and Pound examples do, towards concentration or
condensation of the emotion in the single memorable image. And
what I have said about Lawrence here could, broadly speaking,
be said about Whitman. One is wasting one's time, most of the
time, trying to scan Whitman.

It has been my aim in all chapters of this little book to suggest
a method which the reader can go on applying for himself, rather
than to give exhaustive, and exhausting, lists of examples. Pound
and Eliot are the two greatest masters of one kind of free verse,
Lawrence and Whitman of another. I think I have given the reader
enough information to distinguish one kind from another, and

to help him to apply a tentative metrical analysis to the kind where such analysis is appropriate.

My aim throughout this little treatise has been descriptive rather than prescriptive. I have tried to emphasize the flexibility of the English language, the number of different principles on which verse can be successfully constructed in that language: making one main proviso all through, that no verse is good verse that cannot be spoken aloud naturally by a native English speaker, that is not intimately related to the stress, tone, and pitch patterns of ordinary English speech. Free verse runs more risks than other kinds of English verse, in that it cannot give always such clear and definite clues as regular verse about how the poet would like one to read it aloud (or hear it, of course, in one's head): in recompense, as in the Eliot passage and in the Lawrence passage above, it can at its best get very intimately near the tones of English or American informal speech.

Two Additional Notes

I have given a grossly oversimplified version of this, partly no doubt because of my own difficulties in grasping the complex version. What Epstein and Hawkes say in their pamphlet is that the iambic foot should be redefined as 'weaker-stronger' rather than as 'weak-strong' and that the possibilities of combination are 'weak-weak, weak-tertiary, weak-secondary, weak-primary, tertiary-tertiary, tertiary-secondary, tertiary-primary, secondary-secondary, secondary-primary, primary (single bar) primary, and if one wishes to include the so-called "pause-foot" in which one element of the iamb is a paralinguistic pause (pause) – there are four more possibilities: (pause) weak, (pause) tertiary, (pause, secondary, and (pause) primary, for a total of fourteen possible four-stress matrices for the iambic foot in English, and *no more*.' They can get, however, a great many more, though still a fairly small finite number, by considering the phenomenon of what they call 'juncture' between syllables. They have rather a passion for the number four, and find four kinds of juncture as they find, also, four degrees of pitch. What they mean by juncture can roughly be suggested to the ordinary reader, like myself, by considering the difference between 'Annapolis' and 'An apple is' and 'glass-house' and 'glass house'. It should be noted that their weak-weak combination does not create a true English pyrrhic, nor their tertiary-tertiary, secondary-secondary, or primary-primary combinations a true English spondee. The second element of the foot is always *felt* as stronger. For the purposes of this monograph, I have, though not reverting to the simple binary weak-strong scansion, reduced the Trager-Smith possibilities to: weak-tertiary, weak-secondary, weak-primary: tertiary-secondary, tertiary-primary: secondary-primary, or to six instead of the fourteen Trager-Smith matrices. I have left juncture, as I have left pitch, out of the picture. Epstein and Hawkes do not seem, at least in their monograph of 1956, to be much interested in quantity, which seems to me aesthetically very important in English verse, however difficult it is to write quantitative verse in English that will be taken unambiguously as such. And they do not discuss syllabics.

THE CONCEPT OF STRESS

I have used the word stress in this book for both foot-stress and sentence stress, as also both for word- and phrase-stress and sentence or sense stress. In words and phrases, *hot-water-bottle*, *convict*, *convict*, greater stress is pretty clearly a matter of greater energy or emphasis or loudness of utterance, and, to the ear, of slightly greater prominence. In sense or sentence stress, prominence can sometimes be achieved by pausing, by dropping or lowering the pitch of the voice, by a kind of drawling or lingering rather than by a sort of heightening or tensing: sentence stress is in fact phonetically, or linguistically, a more complicated and various phenomenon than word or phrase stress of the *convict*, *convict* sort. But since the two phenomena are in many ways analogous, and since we do in ordinary speech use the same word for both, I have chosen to use the same word for both, for the sake of clarity to the reader and also, I confess, to help me to feel my own way more easily through my complicated argument. I would note also that I have not used the concept, common in binary concepts of the foot, of non-stress: any syllable that can be uttered has at least minimal stress. I have also emphasized (though this remark might have been more appropriate at the end of the last additional note) that my simplified version of the Trager-Smith four-stress system can always be *translated back* into simple binary stress notation: and that this translation makes many lines of English poetry by, for instance, Milton and Shakespeare much more regular than they at first seem.

Select Bibliography

Prosody is as controversial a subject as theology and it lends itself to a very dry and technical treatment, which many readers find repulsive, bewildering, or both. If one is willing to struggle, however, the drier and more technical books are often the more useful.

The clearest short introduction I know of is JAMES MCAULEY, *Versification*, Michigan State University Press, 1966. Mr McAuley, a distinguished Australian poet, was part author of the spoof on free verse called *Angry Penguins*. He tends to be dismissive about free verse, and not to be much interested in pure stress verse, quantitative verse, or syllabics, but on stress-syllable verse he is interesting.

GEORGE SAINTSBURY'S *A History of English Prosody* in three volumes, condensed in 1910 into *Historical Manual of English Prosody*, is the greatest work in English on the subject. Though Saintsbury perversely chose to scan English verse in longs and shorts, he in fact understood clearly the differences between English and classical versification; his range and taste from the later sixteenth century onward are splendid, though he writes with much less authority about medieval and Old English verse. His highly technical vocabulary is lightened by a very racy, indeed even slangy prose style.

For the modern scientific approach to prosody, I would recommend *Linguistics and English Prosody*, by EDMUND L. EPSTEIN and TERENCE HAWKES, University of Buffalo (Studies in Linguistics: Occasional Papers, 7). With its different symbols for stress, pitch, juncture, and so on, this is hard reading but worth struggling with. I have given a very simplified version of the Trager-Smith system, on which this pamphlet is founded, in this book.

A Linguistic Guide to English Poetry, by GEOFFREY N. LEECH, Longmans Green and Co., London, 1969, covers a much wider field than metrics. It is particularly useful on rhyme.

A Prosody Handbook by the poet KARL SHAPIRO and by ROBERT BEUM, Harper and Row, New York, 1960, is very clear and methodical, and full of illustrative detail.

J. B. LEISHMAN's *Translating Horace*, Bruno Cassirer, Oxford, 1956, is discussed at some length in these pages. Its crisp and witty introduction provides the reader who has little or no Latin with an indispensable 'iron ration' (Leishman's own phrase) of information about classical prosody.

For the reader with little or no Anglo-Saxon, there are two very useful articles in *Essential Articles for the Study of Old English Poetry*, edited by Bossinger and Kahrl, Archon Books, Hamden, Connecticut, 1968. These are MARJORIE DAUNT's 'Old English Verse and English Speech Rhythm' and C. S. LEWIS's 'The Alliterative Metre'.

A difficult but very important book is SEYMOUR CHATMAN, *A Theory of Meter*, Mouton and Co., The Hague, The Netherlands, 1964. Like Epstein, Hawkes, and Leech, Chatman applies modern scientific phonetics to traditional theories of metre. The most interesting chapter is VI, 'Shakespeare's 18th Sonnet: An Experiment in Metrical Analysis'. Twenty-one professors listened to eleven different recordings of this beautiful sonnet, and their metrical analyses ('Shall *I* . . .', '*Shall* I . . .', '*Thou* art . . .', 'Thou *art*') brought out the ambiguities we have noticed more briefly here. Chatman seems to think that there is a real English pyrrhic and a real English spondee, but defined by quantity rather than by stress.

There is no book, so far as I know, and no very substantial article on either pure syllabics or on the rationale of free verse as such, and these are fields that might be promising for a young research student.

Index

Index